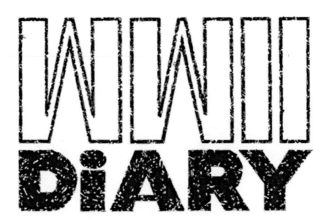

Stories by the Airmen of the
22nd Bomb Squadron
in World War II

David K. Hayward

John A. Johns, Graphic Artist

First Edition 2002
Second Edition 2014

"WWII DIARY: Stories by the Airmen of the 22nd Bomb Squadron in World War II."
Edited by David K. Hayward. First Edition ISBN 0-9656437-2-7. Second Edition ISBN
978-1-62137-460-2.

TABLE OF CONTENTS

DEDICATION

This collection of stories is dedicated to all who served in the 22nd Bomb Squadron in the China-Burma-India Theater in World War II. Special consideration is given to those who did not return and to their families and friends who mourned for them. Lloyd A. Klar, a member of the 22nd Bomb Squadron, expressed these thoughts when he wrote this poem:

SILENT SLEEP

Her great roaring engines are long silent,
Her guns are pitted with rust.
Olive drab paint is flaking and faded,
Turrets are covered with dust.

She sits and waits for her crewmen,
Those young men from another day.
Many long years have passed and gone
Since they all went away.

Where have all those young men gone,
Those boys she knew so well?
They took her there and brought her back,
What stories they can tell.

Some are buried in foreign lands,
War records tell the place.
"Killed in Action" the official words,
Or just "KIA" to save space.

Others went down in a fiery crash,
Just where, no one can tell;

Over Burma jungles or China cliffs
No markers where they fell.

Others came home, the war was over,
We dissipated like the dew,
Then separately we went our ways
Back to the lives we knew.

But in every airman's inner thoughts,
Quiet moments as day ends,
We hear again those engines roar
And voices of our friends.

Now we're aging and almost grey;
Again friends are starting to fall.
They're going now into that long last sleep
That comes one day to us all.

So here's to our fellow comrades,
Those still here or passed away.
We'll remember you as you once were
In a distant place and day.

As we stand here now in silence,
We'll think of you and smile.
Get ready for that final briefing;
We'll join you after a while.

INTRODUCTION

The 22nd Bomb Squadron was activated as a medium bombardment squadron in April 1942, in Columbia, South Carolina. Ground support personnel and some of the aircrews departed from Charleston, South Carolina, aboard the converted luxury liner S.S. Mariposa, in May 1942. After 59 days of plowing through submarine-infested waters, they arrived at Karachi, India, (now Pakistan) in July 1942. Other ships followed with men and materials.

Also, in May 1942, flight crews of the 22nd Bomb Squadron, along with those of the 11th Bomb Squadron, its sister squadron, departed from Morrison Field, Florida, in a flight of twenty-six B-25s. They flew from Florida to South America, across the South Atlantic Ocean, Africa, along the south coast of Arabia and on to Karachi, India. Some went on to China. Three of the original twenty-six B-25s failed to reach India. More planes and crews were to follow along this route to India.

In December 1942, the 22nd Bomb Squadron, with Robert S. Puckett as its first commanding officer, came together as part of the 341st Bomb Group at Chakulia, India, located 100

miles west of Calcutta in eastern India. Replacement crews followed; some flew their B-25s from the States and others traveled by military air transport plane, and the original crews were mighty glad to see them. The 341st bomb group eventually included the 11th, 22nd, 490th and 491st Bomb Squadrons. Air operations by the 22nd began with combat missions flown into Burma and the Bay of Bengal. The goal was to stop the enemy from cutting off the flow of war materials to China.

The squadron moved to Yangkai, China, in January 1944, near Kunming, in the southwesterly part of China, positioned to cut enemy supply lines both overland and at sea, along the China coast. Here, the squadron members became Flying Tigers under General Claire Chennault. At the end of the war, the squadron ceased operations; it was deactivated in November 1945.

PREFACE

The China-Burma-India (CBI) theater of operations during World War II was not given the amount of attention by the outside world that other theaters were given, but the people who served in the CBI were every bit as real as those where more attention was given. This collection of stories brings out the personal side of what it was like to have served in this B-25 squadron in World War II, the 22nd Bomb Squadron of the 341st Bomb Group.

These stories show the reality of events, the sense of duty and determination, the fear, the boredom, and the occasional fun. Many of the stories originated in letters sent home, reflecting the real feelings of the men at the time.

In recent years, with the formation of the 22nd Bomb Squadron Association, some of the stories found their way into the association's quarterly newsletters and its history book entitled *Eagles, Bulldogs & Tigers*, along with illustrations by pilot-artist John A. Johns.

The purpose of this book is to gather, under one cover, all the stories by Steve Stankiewicz, Jim White, Wendell Hanson, and others, and illustrate them with John Johns' artwork.

How many times have we heard, "Grandpa, tell me a story about the war?" Well, here are those stories for the pleasure and memories of grandkids and great-grandkids and all others who are interested in the adventures of those who served in World War II.

ACKNOWLEDGEMENTS

These stories were written by some of the squadron's most gifted storytellers, principally Stephen A. "Steve" Stankiewicz and James M. "Jim" White, both bombardier-navigators, and by pilot Wendell H. Hanson. The clever illustrations and formatting were contributed by another pilot in the squadron, an accomplished graphic artist, John A. Johns, who wrote six stories himself. The editor is David K. "Dave" Hayward, also a 22nd Bomb Squadron pilot. Two of his stories are included as well.

Steve Stankiewicz, Wendell Hanson and Dave Hayward joined the squadron in the spring of 1943, to replace some of the original twenty-six crews. John Johns arrived in August of that year.

By the spring of 1944, Stankiewicz, Hanson and Hayward had completed at least 50 combat missions and were reassigned to duty in the U.S. John Johns completed his combat missions and returned in August of 1944. Jim White, a bombardier-navigator, arrived in India in April 1944, having flown from the U.S. with his crew in a new B-25J. Jim completed his 50 missions and returned to the States in March of 1945.

Additional stories are included, each important in their own way, and all are illustrated by John A. Johns. The introductory poem appearing in the Dedication section was written by 22nd squadron member by Lloyd A. Klar and was first presented by him at a reunion of the 22nd Bomb Squadron at Dayton, Ohio, in 1998. Other authors are Jay V. Percival, Elmer C. "Tommy" Thompson, William H. "Bill" Van Vleck, Chapman M. "Chap" Hale, Jr., Carl A. "Hoot" Gibson and Felix H. "Phil" Speciale.

Stephen A. Stankiewicz
RECOLLECTIONS

People can recall certain dates that stick in their memories, such as where one was when Pearl Harbor was bombed, what one was doing when D-Day in Europe finally arrived, and what the weather was like when the horrible announcement of John F. Kennedy's assassination came over the airwaves.

Similarly, I believe, almost all of us can recall some circumstances the day we left the safety of the USA to begin our long journey to foreign lands and war zones.

Mike Russell and I were the last two to enter the cavernous interior of the commercial plane which was parked on the apron at Miami airport. The plane was manned by civilian airline pilots and they were to take us into the unknown—deliver us to the ultimate adventure of our lives, WAR.

Mike and I paused at the top step and looked back on the country of our birth for one last indelible impression to carry in our minds in the months to come. It was with mixed emotions that we did so. Our feelings ran the gamut of regret, sorrow and overpowering nostalgia.

"Mike, let's take one last look because only God knows when we shall see this again," I said to him. Mike was brusque and cleared his throat. He only said, "Come on Steve," and ducked into the cavernous interior. It would be well over a year  before we saw Miami or home again. The other crews were already deep into poker or other types of games of chance.

For my part, I was leaving parents, school chums, brothers and sisters as well as close relatives, distancing myself from the sort of family closeness so typical of children born of immigrants from eastern European countries. Thoughts of Frankie, my steady gal, brought a lump to my throat. Mike was newly married and his unhappiness showed at the enforced separation from his bride. One can imagine my parents' feeling at that time. One son served in the navy, another with an airborne division, as well as the oldest son who served with the combat engineers; all saw combat around the globe.

Training as teams in the B-25s, the Mitchell bombers at Greenville, South Carolina, our crew consisted of Elmer "Tommy" Thompson, pilot and plane commander; Mike Russell, copilot; me, Steve Stankiewicz, bombardier-navigator; Mike Mihalichko, engineer-gunner; Willard Leuthouser, radio-gunner and Richard Pandorf, rear gunner, who, because of his tender years, we called Dickie Boy.

Originally, we were supposed to fly our own plane from Miami to India via South America, Ascension Island, Khartoum and Arabia to Karachi and then to our base in Chakulia, India.

However, earlier on, one team went down in the Amazon jungle and only one member struggled out safely to civilization after loss of the plane. It was decided by the powers that be that some of the B-25 teams that were to follow would be transported by commercial pilots, at least as far as the coast of India. Eventually, men and machines were reunited in Chakulia, India.

The trip itself was an adventure. Our first real grasp of what we were in for was when we landed in Georgetown, British Guiana, for food and refueling. As we left our plane on the way to the mess hall, several RAF (Royal Air Force) fighters were roaring off the runway, headed out to sea. When we inquired about them we were told that an enemy submarine was sighted off the coast. We were thinking, "A fat lot of good that will do," because none of us saw any bombs under the Spitfires' wings or fuselages and machine guns alone wouldn't do much damage to a sub.

When we got to Natal, Brazil, we were bombarded by lurid stories by the crews who were on their way home after months of overseas service, presumably much of it in combat with the enemy either in China, Burma, India or Africa.

The weather back home was moderate when we left Florida; but it was hot, humid and dusty in Brazil. We were forbidden to leave the base and we heard horrendous stories of Captains, Majors and even Colonels being rounded up in town by the MP's and thrown into jail with the threat of courts-martial ahead.

What their crimes were to merit such harsh treatment we could only guess at, because just going into town and getting a snootfull certainly would not come under the label of criminality. But rumors prevail, no matter where one may be.

It was here that we were indoctrinated and accepted into the Short Snorter Club. We signed all sorts of paper money and in exchange, we got into lively interactions of all sorts; there were all denominations of British, Australian, Indian, Italian, Chinese and Burmese rupees, francs, liras, etc. We had them signed by the military transients passing through the base, some going to combat and some returning from combat. This ritual was repeated as we progressed across the globe and soon we had the Short Snorter bills taped into two and three foot lengths. Not having any such evidence on hand meant surrendering a dollar bill to all and sundry travelers who may have happened to challenge you to produce a Short Snorter. I still have mine and the very first person to sign it was J. C. Sullivan.

Prior to landing at Accra on the Gold Coast of Africa, we stopped briefly at Ascension Island and as we circled that tiny clinker sitting there so pitifully small in that vast blue-green expanse of

Atlantic Ocean. I breathed a sigh of relief that I did not have to navigate our lone B-25 on the trans-Atlantic flight, as my dead reckoning would have had to be flawless and the "piloting" form of navigation can only be used over land. (Although years back Lindbergh made it from Long Island to Paris with no navigational aids except a compass.)

It wasn't until months later that Norm Sloan, one of the navigators in our squadron, made us privy to the intricacies of the sextant and astro compass. I recall that he held a few classes for us at Chakulia and later in Yangkai. Incidentally, I once used the astro compass to get our plane from French Indochina to Kunming.

Our stateside navigation was limited to DR (dead reckoning) and pilotage, and we made training missions to various parts of the country. On one such training trip, weeks before, we had breakfast in Greenville, SC, lunch in Miami and dinner in Washington, DC, and all was accomplished by DR and pilotage.

It was on this trip that we were treated to a comical spectacle of a corporal putting some obviously brand new recruits through close order drill; that was in Miami. Now, the recruits were middle-aged, over-weight, sweating, newly-commissioned captains, majors and lieutenant colonels who gratefully rested momentarily in the shade of a hangar when given "at ease" by their grim-faced taskmaster, a corporal. As he barked "fall in," the group kept on talking and it was something to see and hear the corporal sternly reproaching the officers with "no talking in ranks." He got instant obedience.

The newly commissioned officers were still civilians at heart and they had no idea that they greatly outranked their heartless taskmaster.

They all looked as though they would rather be back behind their desks, in corporate offices, or back in civilian pursuits, but we won the war, all of us combined in a common effort; bank

VPs, tellers, grocery clerks, high school and college students, carpenters, undertakers, electricians, laborers, school teachers and professional athletes from all walks of life and all ages from teens to middle aged patriots, an amalgam of career soldiers, 90-day wonders, reservists and what have you. Evidently, a healthy mixture that worked quite well in the crucible of war.

EARLY WARNINGS

Before leaving the U.S. for overseas duty in early 1943, we were warned about the insect genus "anopheles," fondly remembered as "Anopheles Annie." I paid little heed, however, to the dangers that might be posed by what I thought of as merely an  annoying insect. We were cautioned to wear long-sleeved shirts and to sleep with our mosquito netting properly in place.

I didn't realize that we had much to learn about the hazards to be encountered in foreign lands. Some lessons were learned the hard way and this was to be one of them.

Many of us landed in central Africa on our hegira to do battle with an enemy we didn't know or hadn't even seen. That first night in Africa we were treated to a movie in an open field, an event I eagerly awaited with anticipation. I was wearing a short-sleeved shirt and absent-mindedly swatted at mosquitoes that landed on me and who began to voraciously feed on the exposed parts of my anatomy. After a while, it just got to be too much for me so I headed for my tent early and went to bed—to heck with the movie.

I kept a canteen full of a lemon drink under my cot. Sometime during the night, feeling thirsty, I reached for the canteen for a sip. After a while, I felt a funny sensation on my arms and lips. I snapped on my flashlight and was horrified when I saw the canteen; a mass of ants and revolting bugs crawled around the neck of the canteen, and nasty looking creatures were a living blanket in the area around the cot. I danced around, shaking off ants and bugs that were crawling over my face, neck and arms.

They warned us to not keep any kind of edibles or potables where unwanted guests could get at them. And, don't eat or drink in the dark. If you can't see it, leave it alone. (This philosophy underwent a radical change later.)

With short stops in Khartoum, Aden, Masirah Island and Karachi, we eventually arrived at our base on the outskirts of that "great" metropolis, Chakulia, India. During that first week of orientation, I managed to put in a training flight with Mike Russell, pilot, shooting landings. I even participated in a bombing mission over Burma.

But then, things got a bit hairy. One evening, while coming back from the officers club, a sudden weakness overcame me and I began to shake uncontrollably; I was barely able to crawl into my sack.

Mike Russell and Elmer Thompson stopped by to see what I was up to. When they saw me under the covers shivering and shaking they prevailed upon two doctors to come look at me—they were transients, just passing through for assignment at some point beyond. After a cursory examination, they started to leave, meanwhile leaving the mosquito netting draped over the T-bar, exposing me to the mercy of flying insects and mosquitoes. When Mike began to solicitously put the netting around my mattress, one of the doctors said, "Never mind, he already has malaria. Just call the chop-wagon." Well, the doctor was only half right; the final diagnosis was malaria AND amoebic dysentery.

When I first arrived at the hospital complex, there was a captain in a bed across the room from me and he was either sound asleep or unconscious. I passed out and awoke much later to the tune of a clanking water pump. Looking out of the window, I saw a pump wallah manning the pump and supplying water for the whole complex. Dressed in just a turban and a rag around his midriff, perspiration running off his face and torso in rivulets, his rhythmic up and down movement never varied—his stamina was astounding.

I asked a corpsman, "What happened to the captain?" In return I got a breezy, "Oh, he died." I didn't want to believe that and said so, but received no denial or affirmation. I decided then and there that I wanted to get the hell out of there, and demanded my clothes. He only said to me, "Talk to the nurse."

She came and told me that I was in no fit condition to get out of bed and not to make trouble. Further, she said she would call the doctor and he would set me straight. I retorted, "Baloney, nobody outranks a patient."

"We shall see," she replied.

In a little while the doctor came in (a lieutenant colonel); he was a no nonsense guy and wracked me back unmercifully. (Has anybody ever tried to appear at stiff attention while lying on his back and answering, "Yes sir, no sir, yes sir," innumerable times?) He knew what he was doing in keeping me in the hospital, as I was far from well. Sleep was impossible. On a sheet of paper I had to mark an "X" each time I rushed to the toilet in answer to the call of nature. In time the "X's" became less and less frequent and finally I was discharged, sporting a healthy-looking tan, thanks to the numerous atabrine tablets I had to ingest for days on end.

It was a very subdued second louie who left the hospital on that hot, sunny day.

As time went on, I found out there were many other things to learn about that exotic country. It was, after all, a land of bats and bugs, Bengal tigers and jackals, mongoose and cobras, stifling heat and drenching rains, rich Brahmins and dirt poor untouchables, beggars and sheiks, a land of wealth and poverty, myriad contrasts and predictable periods of starvation, with big cities and tiny villages, urban areas abutting wild jungles.

The India I saw was mostly a one-crop farming countryside; rice paddies pockmarked the country. During the dry season, many a rice paddy substituted as a landing strip for crippled aircraft returning from bombing missions over Burma. (All landings were not perfect.)

"All this too shall pass," I comforted myself—"Sooner or later I shall see my home and family again."

NIGHT GREMLINS

As I lay there on my cot, the pitch-black night was not conducive to restful sleep. The cacophony of yodeling jackals added to my discomfort and restlessness. Mysterious noises and slithering sounds kept me wary and alert. (Was that the sound of a cobra moving across the floor? And what was that strange sound under my cot??)

I was a new arrival in Chakulia in early 1943 and unseen and unknown dangers crowded my mind. My Colt 45 automatic under my pillow was of little comfort. I did not even have the luxury of having my roomie Ellsworth Valentine in the next cot as he was away somewhere in his duties as our assistant finance officer.

I felt it would be extremely dangerous for me to fall asleep and become prey to the wild animals lurking in every corner. My imagination ran riot, making sleep impossible.

Sometime during the night the moon came out from behind clouds and bathed the room with an eerie glow. Now I was sure I saw a tiger just outside my room, and wasn't that a hyena slavering and eyeing me as a possible meal? In my mind's eye I was sure I was seeing animals that didn't even exist in India. (How come I even placed a black-maned African lion in my room?)

How I wished that I was now back in my old home town strolling down Broadway and flirting with the girls—oh, to see a street lamp again—and sidewalks and a drugstore with its marble-topped soda fountain.

But all that was so far away and unattainable and I was left to deal with all my bugaboos for some time to come.

It is amazing how one can become acclimated to any given circumstance. In no time at all, various terrors were dissipated and walking in the dark from one place to another was no longer fearful and fraught with terror. Running to the toilet in the dark of night wearing just flip-flops and shorts became routine and held no terrors for us. Our ever-present Colt 45's gave us a feeling of invincibility.

The only thing to be feared would be an occasional rabid jackal running through our living area. We found out that, in most cases, wildlife avoided humans. (I didn't believe this sort of behavior applied to man-eating tigers, however.) Back in those days it was reported that cobras killed 100,000 junglees in isolated villages annually. Not very comforting news to us, I must say.

We lucky ones survived bullets and bombs, fighter planes and anti-aircraft fire, malaria and dysentery, hellish heat rash and scary landings, bugs and beetles, spiders and scorpions, and in all this we made fast friends and gained enough reminiscences to last a lifetime.

The greatest feeling of all was to step on United States soil once again and greet family, friends and sweethearts.

That warm glow is still palpable after these many years.

BENGAL LANCERS

In my occasional prowling around our Chakulia Air Base, I once ran across some natives drawing water out of a deep well. The bucket at the end of the rope took an interminable time to come into view—and no wonder—the rope attached to the bucket was at least one hundred feet long; it was hard to recognize a well that deep. In questioning a native who spoke some English, I received a bit of startling news; the well, he told me, was dug by the famed Bengal Lancers many years before and it was supposedly in the center of their fort. In a fever of excitement, I began exploring the area and soon discovered remnants of brick walls overgrown with weeds.

I reconstructed the fort in my mind; here were remains of barracks, there a suitable distance away were crumbling stalls for horses; even a partial wall was still standing, containing a window frame with rusting iron bars still attached—a mute reminder that even in those days there were some soldiers that screwed up and served time in the stockade. One just can't imagine any soldier wanting to go AWOL (absent without leave)

in such a dry and barren countryside, with villages of any size few and far between.

Still in the grip of excitement I visualized long lines of Sepoys marching four abreast, shepherded by officers on horseback, while bringing up the rear trundled the cannons, followed by supply wagons raising clouds of dust miles long.

All of the information that I obtained about the area, I included in a letter home. Much, much later I discovered that the letter was censored and all of the interesting bits of history I gleaned were heartlessly cut out and could not be shared with those back home, unfortunately.

On another hiking trip Mike Russell and I chanced upon a dump, where all the mess hall garbage from our base was dumped into an open pit; uneaten scraps of food were a magnet for poor, starving natives. Men, women and children stood knee deep in that awful mess, each salvaging pieces of bread, vegetables, strands of spaghetti, etc., and carefully placing them in cartons, tin cans or any receptacle they may have had at hand.

In between rice harvests, food was scarce and starvation was a fact of life for these poor, hungry people. Pity, rather than revulsion, was the emotion one felt. But these country folk were much better off than those homeless masses in the cities.

The rains that often overflowed the riverbanks created a bonanza as the waters invaded dried-up rice paddies, bringing with it small fish that were easily netted and which provided much needed food to supplement what little food they had.

The villagers stretched netting between trees, high up in the crowns, to snag bats flying during the night hours.

Native transients seem to have free rein through our barracks area, and as we were used to seeing Indians repairing roads, we thought little of mango-wallahs and cha-wallahs vending their wares to the native workers.

The products were carried on their heads, the fruits in baskets and tea in red clay pots. The mangoes were tasty when ripe but acted as a cathartic, an unwelcome condition and something to be avoided. With a cup dangling from a waist band, the cha-wallah dispensed the tea to his customers after first wiping the inside of the cup with a dirty rag. (This was a stupendous sanitary precaution, I might add.)

Walking about the countryside was a respite from long hours of inactivity; it helped chase boredom and occasionally rewarded us with interesting experiences.

On one such foray, Mike Russell and I were accosted by a young Indian boy who we judged to be about ten or eleven years of age. He seemed fascinated by our side arms and by animated gestures urged us to shoot at various targets he pointed out, but we declined. As we walked along, he motioned to a falcon perched on a limb high up in a tree and frantically urged us to shoot it. We refused and he disappointedly went away. Besides, it would be embarrassing to miss, which we were sure to do.

As we trudged along, a water buffalo noticed us and started toward us, nose up, horn and ears laid back. I said, "Mike, he looks like he is ready to charge." There was no place to run so we decided to shoot the beast if need be. "You shoot him in the nose and I'll hit him in the eye; a bullet will just bounce off his skull," I informed my intrepid friend.

This was ludicrous, to say the least, as my marksmanship was not one of my strong points. Just a week or two before, T. J. Smith had brought a few of us to the firing range to fire our Colt 45's at life-size silhouettes. I emptied a clip and while I was reloading, Smitty went to look at the target.

"How did I do?" I asked when he returned.

"Let's put it this way," he said, "if that was the enemy he'd never walk again. You shot away his ankles." Well, I couldn't visualize stopping a one ton bull by hitting his hooves, so we were in big trouble.

The bull was picking up speed as he came on and panic best describes my feelings. Just then, a little brown boy, waving a foot-long twig, ran at the bull and hitting it on the nose, he diverted the animal, which ran off obediently, much to our relief. The wetness on my lower extremities was more than perspiration you may be sure.

Just another day in Chakulia.

TIGER, TIGER........

Late each afternoon the tootling of a faraway fife could be heard, growing louder and louder as a ragtag band of old retired British Army Sepoys drew nearer and passed my hut on their way to the airstrip to do guard duty at the revetments. Their leader rendered an "eyes left" and a snappy salute as the contingent passed by, armed with six foot long bamboo poles, their shoulders squared and marching in perfect cadence, lent dignity to the barefoot guards. Despite raggedy khaki shorts, worn bush jackets and torn parts of old uniforms, the beribboned veterans sported medals of various sizes and shapes which were worn proudly and attested to their loyal service to the "Raj" many years ago.

Perhaps here I should describe the architecture of our huts where we lived and slept, with our GI trunks (foot lockers) containing all of our worldly possessions in a corner on the cement floor. Cots with the inevitable mosquito netting draped from wooden T-frames over our beds further graced the room. The walls were made of a paste of mud and cow dung spread over bamboo matting and, when dried, were whitewashed, effectively sealing in all sorts of bugs, termites and maggots. The ceiling was whitewashed burlap, which also was home to a host of interesting denizens that chirped, flew and hopped. The occasional falling insect bothered us not at all.

The window frames and door openings were bereft of windows and doors (sort of primitive air conditioning). The roof was made of rice straw held in place by bamboo slats. There were three rooms to a hut. Front and back porches were made of cement and, roofed over, provided a place to sit when the sun went down.

As for the afore-mentioned guards, I had no idea who provided them and was mystified who paid them or if they got paid at all. Some wag in our group named them "Tanda pani wallahs," loosely translated, "The Cold Stream Guards."

I drew officer of the day in Chakulia one time in early 1943, and it was a memorable event. Accompanied by an MP sergeant and a Jeep driver, we proceeded to drive around the perimeter of the base and I saw places I didn't know existed. In the fast-falling light I saw a clearing filled with brightly colored mustard and lewisite bombs, row upon row, uncounted numbers of malevolence. They were never used but were a deterrent for all to see.

Continuing on, we spotted a flickering light in the jungle. As we drew near, three or four natives with bamboo poles could be seen huddled around a small fire. These were our brave guards who had marched so proudly just a short time before.

I got out of the Jeep and picked my way through the brush, getting madder by the minute, thinking, "Why weren't they at the revetments guarding the planes?" Looking fearfully at the surrounding jungle they conveyed to me they were terrorized of a tiger that had killed a bullock on our airstrip and had supposedly killed and eaten a native boy near a small village.

Whether true or not, I made them leave the questionable safety of their tiny fire and chased them to the revetment area where the worst danger they'd face would most likely be nosy natives driven by simple curiosity.

Our idyllic living was frequently interrupted by air tours over Burma where, for mystifying reasons, we were shot at as we brought 500-pound gifts to Tojo's minions.

Just another little something to write home about. Oh well— c'est la guerre.

DACOITS

Among the unsavory segments of the Indian population were the dacoits. One day I managed to obtain a copy of a Calcutta newspaper that was printed in English. It had a story in it that described the depredations by dacoits, which I found out were roving bands of thieves and murderers.

One day Lt. Ellsworth Valentine, our assistant finance officer (my roomie) informed us, "There will be no pay day this month." His office was in a small building in an isolated part of our air base and it was ransacked by a person or persons unknown during the night. The safe contained our wages and it had disappeared. We could not envision thin, undernourished natives being able to manhandle and carry away a bulky, extremely heavy safe.

So, it must have been done by an organized band of Indian gangsters (the dacoits), well supplied with tools of the trade needed to force open the large safe; also, a truck must have been used to haul the cumbersome vault far into the jungle where it could be hacked and opened without fear of detection. Much later, it was found open and empty.

Base personnel not otherwise employed were ordered by the CO (commanding officer) to go into the surrounding fields and jungle to look for the safe; we were instructed to go into the boondocks, side by side, in a long thin line and not to lose sight of one another on either side of us. One other precautionary measure was to remember to keep directional reference to the sun, which was fine except that very few of us noted in which direction of travel we first entered the scrubby landscape.

25

Everything went well for some time, as we hooted and hollered every once in a while, until we noticed there were no answering responses. In time, the guys on either side of me disappeared also. I thrashed around and came upon a "junglee" family busily working at their rice harvest.

I got interested in watching them slapping sheaves of rice plants against a slanted, shiny board, loosening the grains of rice which slid down into a heap onto a tarpaulin.

An hour flew by and it was time to get going. Asking these people the way to Chakulia was a study in futility as they had no idea of directions or what I was saying to them.

I began walking in a direction I thought would bring me back to the base or perhaps to the village. As I kept walking, slapping at bugs and mosquitoes, I swore at myself for not thinking to bring my pocket compass with me.

Night was rapidly approaching and I was beginning to feel concerned. I came upon a fallen tree in a glen and sat down upon it to orient myself and assess the situation. Very shortly after, I heard thrashing off to one side.

Hoping I didn't disturb a sleeping tiger, two sergeants came into view. When they spied me they whooped in delight; one said to the other, "Hey, it's okay, here's a navigator and he'll get us out of this mess." I hated to tell them that I was hopelessly lost and could be of no help to anyone.

So we decided to stick together and started out bravely into the dark which suddenly enveloped us. Night fell swiftly and completely with no moon or stars showing. Once again, we managed to get separated and lost sight and sound of each other. Stumbling in the dark, I heard the sound of a cow bell and headed for the sound. As I drew closer I spotted a swinging light, which I saw was a kerosene lantern hanging on the back end of a

bullock cart. I scared the hell out of the native leading his animal as I suddenly appeared noisily out of the jungle. With not so much as a "by your leave" I hopped on to the cart, not caring where we were heading just so long as we got to a village, any village, where I could find someone who spoke English and where I might find transportation back to the base.

Sure enough, we arrived back in Chakulia where a ten-wheeler was parked on a dusty road, waiting for stragglers limping in from the jungle.

I met Sulli (Jim Sullivan) and his classic remark, "You shoulda stayed in bed," still rings in my ears.

P.S. Although the story of the robbery is true, Art Lynch informed me much later that the dastardly deed was perpetrated by two American sergeants. That kind of deflated me as I was sure we had experienced an unwelcome visit by the well-known but infamous dacoits.

EXCITING TIMES

Not far from our shack was our toilet, which was a slit trench with a board raised above it, with appropriate holes spaced along its length.

This was surrounded by a low wall with an entrance at one end and little else. Sitting there in broad daylight we were a comic sight to the native men and women passing by, going about their business of repairing the dirt roads washed out by the monsoon rains.

We finally had the structure roofed over and screened, which gave us all a modicum of privacy.

Before we got used to Indian cookery many of us were afflicted with a gripping stomach disorder which we called the GIs (pronounced Gee Eyes). This condition can best be described as, "Quick, run to the toilet," a dozen or more times a day. Inasmuch as some days (or nights), one had to run, but fast, to the toilet at mother nature's insistence; it became a good substitute for jogging, a very healthy activity. (Every cloud has a silver lining.)

On one such dark night I headed for the John, with my Colt 45 strapped around my waist. As I walked up the pathway, I heard a snuffling and felt something wet touching the back of my leg just above the top of my Chukka boot. I

stopped, turned around, and in the light of my flashlight saw a grinning jackal about two feet from me.

It was his cold, wet nose against the back of my leg that startled me. I aimed a kick at the impudent rascal and it scooted into the

brush as my Chukka boot flew off my foot and went sailing in a graceful arc into the darkness.

But there was no time to go looking for it as urgent business had to be attended to. So—on to the John.

Mike Russell and Elmer Thompson were already ensconced on their thrones, and by the light of a kerosene lantern, were solemnly reading from ragged pieces of old newspaper and torn magazines, pieces of which would shortly be utilized in a more mundane manner.

We three sat in silence, and while we were engrossed in reading, I was mesmerized in watching a life and death struggle

between a large black ant and a huge fly on the floor between my feet. But then I heard a rustle overhead and looked up—a long brown snake wrapped around a ceiling pole was staring down at me—contemplatingly I thought. It took me a second or two to react. I jumped up and yelled frantically, "SNAKE!!!"

Mike and Elmer's reaction time was superb. Without a moment's hesitation they jumped up in unison with lightening speed to the same height. It was a magnificent leap from a sitting position.

This was enough frantic activity for the snake and it slithered away to safety. I thought of shooting at it but thought

better. It wouldn't be wise to shoot at a
moving target at two o'clock in the
morning and wake up sleeping comrades in
nearby huts.

Meanwhile, back to the struggling
antagonists; the ant won. It was hauling
away its victim as I watched the dramatic finish of the fray.

We three stalwarts stumbled back to our shack perchance to
sleep while awaiting another attack of the GIs.

Ho hum—just another night in "exciting" Chakulia, India.

MILITARY CENSORSHIP

One of the most distasteful duties to perform, in my mind, was censoring mail. But, in order to dispel the feeling that I was prying into peoples' personal business I made it a point not to look at names on the letters, neither the senders' nor the recipients'.

However, it must be told that this occasional duty was not without its lighter moments; particularly when one ran across letters obviously written by either a truck driver or other ground support personnel. The incorrect flight terms used were a clue and their lurid reports of missions that I had been on were certainly incompatible with the actual facts. But, in every case, the description of the air battles with Japanese Zero fighters held me enthralled.

The writers usually embellished the stories to sweethearts and families and were not modest by any means—at times they appeared to put the Red Baron of World War I to shame by their accounts of fictional daring accounts. Here and there the writers sprinkled in such names as Thazi Junction, Mandalay, Schwebo, etc., which added color to the stories. And I, the censor, added credence to the stories by dutifully cutting out the names of targets mentioned and so colorfully described.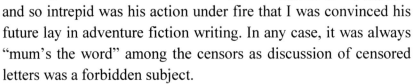

It so happened that I ran across a letter written by a young truck driver known to me, and his description of a bombing mission was so full of suspense and so intrepid was his action under fire that I was convinced his future lay in adventure fiction writing. In any case, it was always "mum's the word" among the censors as discussion of censored letters was a forbidden subject.

But, I couldn't help but wonder how those intrepid knights of the skies explained their lack of Air Medals and DFC's which were certainly warranted if the accounts of their brave actions were to be believed by those at home.

A WALK IN THE WOODS

In mid-1943 we were periodically bombing at targets in Burma just often enough to keep us sharp. Occasionally, things slacked off and consequently many of us tended to grow lethargic and bored.

To keep busy we drew assignments other than flying duty such as officer of the day, censoring mail or other seemingly inconsequential details. In my spare time I compiled a booklet of known targets as well as possible targets, with information as to location (latitude and longitude), course, distance and the target altitude above sea level.

This didn't take up too much of my time so I had lots of time to wander around the "neighborhood" poking into things that were none of my business but turned out to be unusual and informative, now and then.

One day the commanding officer routed us out (figuratively) and had us tramping the countryside en masse for much needed exercise. As far as I could determine there was no one in charge of the detail so we more or less followed whoever happened to be in front of the pack.

 We were well in the bush when we came to a clearing where, in the distance, we spied a herd of cattle. Off to one side there was a dust cloud which, upon our getting closer, turned out to be two bulls fighting for supremacy. The other bullocks paid no heed to the battle.

The bulls stopped after a while to rest, I presumed, when one of the antagonists spotted us and started to trot our way. Most of us who only saw pictures of cows and bulls began to run, scattering in all directions and not really caring to see the live animals up close.

One of the guys (I forgot his name) who I always thought of as the Oklahoma cowboy stood his ground, calmly took off his bush jacket and advanced toward the oncoming bull. Waving his jacket and letting out cowboy yells caused the bull to pull up short. The bull looked upon our cowboy friend and decided to withdraw. It then trotted back to his cows only to resume his battle with his male adversary.

Just like in the movies, I fell and whacked my nose on a rock. As I lay there, drops of blood fell on a flat stone whose color and texture caught my attention. "Gee," I thought to myself, "the stones here in India are no different than those near the clay pits of Sayreville, New Jersey." I don't know why this came as a surprise to me.

Somewhat rejuvenated, we continued our walk and eventually got back to the air base. Amazingly, I noticed marks of "civilization" in the uninhabited region—lying on the ground, empty sardine cans, match books, cigarette packs (empty) and various kinds of tin cans and food cartons could be seen here and there.

Evidently litter bugs know no boundaries and are not restricted just to Americans back home.

INDIAN JUSTICE
COUNTRY STYLE

In one of my forays into the hinterlands of India, and copiously perspiring in the blazing heat, I chanced upon an amazing incident. I was trudging off the road into a clearing that was overgrown with low bushes here and there.

I noticed a shed-like structure with a tin roof baking in the sun, and a short distance away a contingent of Indians had stopped and set about placing folding chairs near a square-topped table. They seemed to defer respectfully to a tall turbaned individual. He looked and acted as a personage of high estate, a fact that would be impressed on me shortly.

He seated himself upon an ornate arm chair that was brought forth by a couple of his flunkies. One of the coterie then held an umbrella over the big shot's head to protect him from the fierce rays of the sun, as he seated himself at the table. He then gestured imperiously and another person of the company, who stood in the back, left and approached the shed from which came piteous sobs and wails. "Surely," I thought to myself, "they couldn't possibly have a human being incarcerated in that small hut in undoubtedly suffocating and killing temperature?" But this apparently was the local poky. The padlock was removed, the door opened and a trembling miscreant appeared and was led before the august presence seated at the table.

Then it dawned on me—this was a traveling judge, and court was in session. An accuser came forth and seemed to have a lot of bad things to say about the poor wretch crying and shaking in front of the judge. A sharp word from the judge and the sniveling stopped instantly.

The accuser finished his complaint and the judge motioned to the accused to make a statement. The accused had his say and then the judge held up his hand for silence. He appeared to be cogitating and, after a short while, he rendered his decision.

The accused leaped up off his knees and with yelps of joy he bounded out of sight. The accuser didn't appear to be too happy with the decision and without another word he too left, shoulders drooping. The judge wrapped his long cloak about himself and started off. The others went about gathering the paraphernalia and followed the judge out of sight.

Justice had been served and that "Judge Bean of the Boondocks" was on his way to other areas where he would dispense justice, when and where needed.

I marveled at the quick and final decision of that barefoot native judge; no appeals, no lawyers, no endless arguments, just instant, raw and final justice.

As the company wended its way, one could almost hear the judge say, "Case closed."

AROUND THE CAMP

The 22nd Bomb Squadron members celebrated the squadron's first anniversary in India. Sgt. Roberts didn't have time to bake a cake so he used two loaves of bread, which he covered with shaving lather to make it look like cake.

I can still picture "Beans" Campbell, a happy-go-lucky pink-cheeked cherub. I can almost hear him calling out to me outside my hut, "Hey, Stinky, get out of the sack, you just volunteered for a mission."

I recall the occasional movies that were shown outdoors, where we sat on rocks or whatever was available, and the natives materialized out of the darkness and sat or stood, enthralled as the action unfolded on the screen.

At one of those showings, Joe Baldanza livened up the proceedings when he rode a snorting bullock through the audience. He sure was one happy-go-lucky guy.

PALM SUNDAY
PREPARATION FOR EASTER

Mike Russell and I were given passes and we entrained for Jamshedpur. We had purchased tickets earlier at the Chakulia railroad station. While waiting for the train we noticed two waifs, a little native boy and a still tinier girl, apparently brother and sister. They were physically in the last stages of starvation, their plight ignored by the people waiting to board the next train. The children's stomachs were distended and their sunken eyes and pipe-stem arms and legs were sure signs that they had not eaten in quite some time.

On noting this, Mike (good soul that he is) went to a vendor who was cooking some flat cakes in boiling oil on a makeshift coke burning stove and he purchased some cakes, which he then gave to the children. They silently accepted the food and then held the gifts; they made no effort to eat. Just then, an English cleric approached us and said, "These children, as so many others, are beyond help. You can do nothing to alleviate their hunger as they are unable to chew and swallow food. You cannot feed all of India." This fact of life we found hard to accept but could do nothing about it.

It was apparently market day in Jamshedpur as we spied a junglee family headed for the marketplace. Leading the pack was a fierce-looking man, armed with a spear and bow and arrows carried on his back. Following him was his wife, carrying a huge bundle of goods for trading; next came a little boy balancing another large bundle on his head with the family dog bringing up the rear.

Mike and I arrived at our destination after much effort, walking dusty roads while perspiring profusely. We stumbled upon the cottage where the Patna missionary lives. Mike and I had nothing to eat or drink since the day before, in preparation for communion.

The good Father was aghast when we told him of our long fast and he immediately set about making a pot of tea, searching his sparse cupboard for something to feed us. The lone tea bag that he found, plus a stale cupcake he forced upon us, served our immediate needs for our hunger and thirst.

After taking care of our religious needs he then sat back and plied us with questions. We brought him up to date on several topics and then it was story-telling time.

He seemed so happy to talk to someone other than poor natives that our visit with him lasted a couple of hours. He reminisced on what his life was like 50 or 60 years ago.

With a faraway look in his eyes he told many stories, some adventuresome and some stark and frightening, that were a part of life to the jungle natives he ministered to.

He told us about his early days in India and some adventures he experienced. In those early days, his cottage was in the midst of a jungle where many confrontations with Bengal tigers took place. In those early days, tigers took a fearful toll of the natives.

One story that stands out most in my mind is his tale of a near fatal confrontation with a man-eating tiger. Although the event occurred many years ago, it was still vivid in his memory.

One day when he was returning to his cottage after ministering to jungle natives of a far off village, he strode along a jungle trail and soon sensed that he was being followed. When he turned around to see what it was, he saw a huge tiger stalking him. The missionary sprinted to his cottage, into his home and slammed and bolted the door just in time as the tiger's heavy body hit the door with such force that it almost came off the hinges.

But that was not the end of it. That man-eater prowled and growled all night long, every once in a while hurling itself at the door. Luckily, the door held up under the continuous assault by the hungry tiger. Finally, the tiger gave up his vigil and left at dawn.

This good man, as well as other ministers of various beliefs, brought civilization, hope and solace into otherwise drab lives.

EASTER SUNDAY
AND CHAPLAIN CLARE

The Chakulia, India, air base of 1943 was an airstrip with a control tower plus one or two nondescript buildings by brush and tangled jungle, close to a native village. Our living quarters were a short distance away and the whole consisted of thatched-roof huts, mess halls, a hospital compound, supply depot, etc., all prudently situated some distance away from each other to prevent destruction by one well-placed enemy bomb. It was quite a spread. Frequent rains necessitated road work, and native workers were constantly occupied making needed repairs.

Easter Sunday dawned, sunny and hot. Many of us gathered in a bench-lined hut and eagerly awaited the Patna Mission Father to celebrate Mass, as many of us were unable to attend such services on a regular basis. In our gathering were aerial gunners, radiomen, mechanics, pilots, nurses and bombardiers, plus a native or two.

We all sat quietly, each with his or her thoughts, and after a while we all began to fidget.

As we sat there in disappointment, Chaplain Thomas H. Clare came in and greeted us. He told us that he received word that the missionary could not make it to our base as he conducted services at villages along the way and would be detained for hours.

As we prepared to leave the hut, Chaplain Clare, even though not of our faith, asked us if we minded if he conducted services for

us. We were all Catholics but were more than pleased to have him lead us in prayer to celebrate that holy day. Finally, after a short homily and readings from the Good Book, the Chaplain ended the services. We thanked him effusively and marveled at the goodness of that fine man.

There, in a faraway land in a hut near a jungle, we practiced ecumenism long before it became a fashion to do so. I think we all learned a good lesson that day.

Epilogue: The members of the 22nd Bomb Squadron and the entire 341st Bomb Group loved, respected and admired this fine man, Chaplain Clare. Unfortunately, he never made it back to the USA. The final story was written by Chick Marrs Quinn in his book "Aluminum Trail" as follows:

25 May 1944, B024 #0184, Yangkai, Dead: 10

This 14th Air Force aircraft from the 373rd Bomb Squadron, 308th Bomb Group, departed Yangkai, China, intended destination Chabua, India, on a ferry mission. At last radio contact they were 30 minutes east of Chabua. This was the last time this aircraft or crew was heard from. Due to the mountainous terrain where the plane was lost, it is believed if the plane were located, it would be all but impossible to recover the remains. The crew of this aircraft was declared dead as of 26 May 1944, missing in flight since 25 May 1944, between Yangkai, China, and Chabua, India.

Capt. Thomas H. Clare, a passenger on this plane, was from the 341st Bomb Group.

COCA COLA
AND STRANGE FRUIT

In the hottest part of the season in Chakulia, India, the air base received a shipment of gallon jugs filled with cola syrup. It was up to us to find a bottling plant to process this precious liquid into delectable Coca Cola. A contingent, myself included, led by Elmer "Tommy" Thompson proceeded to a soda plant where a deal was struck with the plant owner. I believe the bottler was to receive a part of the product as his payment. We visited the plant and it appeared to me that it hadn't been used in years. But if that rusted equipment could do the job that was all right with us.

I wouldn't say that the equipment was antiquated and not recently used, but capping the bottles of soda used prehistoric capping techniques. The bottles, after being filled, were capped at the neck with a rubber gasket and a glass ball snapped into place and held with spring tension. This method was used in place of metal caps. The plant owner was expected to know how much soda or seltzer was to be used.

We found out later that the glass balls were not very good at keeping the fizz in the bottles. He did not use rubber gaskets and so what we got was a brown, unappetizing liquid made doubly unpalatable for lack of ice to cool the drink. We did not have the luxury of ice or refrigeration on the base.

After negotiations with the plant owner were completed, he gave us a tour of his orchards. He was particularly proud of his lemon, lime, banana and orange trees. Evidently, no one, especially his caretakers, were allowed to eat the fruit. All the

53

trees were considered to be decorative shrubs and the fruit was allowed to drop and rot on the ground.

There was one particular tree that had a large pineapple-like fruit hanging in abundance. No one was allowed to touch them, but the owner personally presented one of the fruits to us. None of the other fellows wanted it, so I inherited the  item. That fruit was treated as something rare and desirable, and the natives appeared envious of me for getting such a prize.

I brought the fruit to my hut and placed it on a bench near the doorway to my room. My bearer, Vade, spotted it and his eyes lit up. He assured me that it was a rare and delectable fruit. I said, "Okay, Vade, open it," as I handed him my knife. He stood the fruit on end and cut the top off and immediately there was an odor that repelled me.

I said, "Vade, it's rotten."

"Oh, no, Sahib, it is goot." When I got over the initial shock of the smell, I looked into the center of the fruit; swimming in the center in a milky fluid were tightly packed, large, almond shaped, cream colored objects. I told Vade to eat some, which he gladly did. He fished one out and ate the fleshy part of the fruit and spat out the pit.

He smacked his lips and ate another, and another. I was intrigued and decided to try one while holding my nose. As soon as I popped the malodorous object into my mouth, instantly my sense of taste was overcome with different kinds of pleasant flavor. I detected sweet orange, concord grapes, peaches and banana and other delightful taste sensations. Vade looked so longingly at the football-sized fruit that I impulsively told him to take it home to his family. Although Vade told me the name of the fruit, I have forgotten it long ago. But I still remember how surprised I was by the taste of what I thought to be spoiled fruit.

As an aside, it was at that plant owner's estate where I saw one of his native workers continuously toss a clinking chamois bag from one hand to the other. I asked him why he was doing that. He untied the bag and revealed newly minted silver rupees and bits of silver gleaming on the inside of the bag, which were removed at the end of the day with quicksilver.

His master went to the bank daily and procured more new silver rupees, trading in the old. Then, the activity was repeated for the purpose of knocking bits of silver and trapping them in the chamois bag. I presumed this procedure produced perhaps thirty cents worth of silver trapped in the chamois bag, so one can imagine what a munificent salary the native got for his day-long efforts.

I suppose this activity kept the native off the streets begging for pice and annas. But working for a living lent dignity to his life.

STEVE AND THE SCORPION

I awoke in total darkness. It must have been between four and five o'clock in the morning and several crews were scheduled to be briefed by Sibley at 0600 hours, me included.

I yawned loudly and this woke up my roomie, Ellsworth Valentine.

Val rested on one elbow and watched silently as I made preparations for departure. He said not a word until I reached for my shoes. "Stop," he said sharply. "Shake them out. You never know what could be in them."

I shook one shoe and nothing happened. Then I shook the other shoe and there was the sound of something hitting the cement floor.

By the light of my flashlight I spied the granddaddy of all scorpions. He waved his claws in a menacing manner and held his barbed tail at the ready. And he stayed there and did not retreat. He actually challenged me as if to invite combat. The beastie had some nerve, I thought.

Meanwhile, I had put on my clod-hoppers, so I was ready for combat. I kicked the scorpion across the room and it skidded to a stop under Val's cot. I don't think Val appreciated that, as Val's brogans were there under the cot, an inviting hiding place for our belligerent opponent. I didn't wait to see what happened next as my date with the enemy had to be kept.

But Val was an easy-going guy and I don't think he would reciprocate by putting something slithery under my pillow in my absence. However, just to be on the safe side, I shook out my cot nightly before retiring.

But, as a well-known comic used to say, "One never know, do one?"

SNOW STORM

As I stood in the doorway of my hut, an astonishing sight met my eyes. The sun was high in the sky and mid-morning heat was already suffocating. I spied what appeared to be snowflakes in the distance and the whole white mass seemed to be drawing nearer.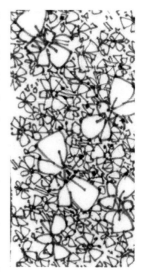

But–how could that be? At that hour, the sun had the temperature soaring close to 100 degrees.

As I stood there, mesmerized, the reason for the white cloud (of what I thought to be falling snowflakes) turned out to be white moths, millions upon millions of them, and they passed overhead in a huge cloud and into the jungle beyond.

As quickly as they appeared, they just as quickly disappeared into nothingness beyond our air base. I have never seen such a sight before or since.

As the Christmas season was approaching, I felt for a moment that I was witnessing a miracle of snowfall in temperatures rivaling that of a hothouse.

But Christmas came and went and visions of fields covered with snow became just a memory of days gone by. Home and family became just fleeting thoughts of things and places far, far away.

As I stood there, I was assailed with feelings of sadness and nostalgic yearnings for something nebulous I could not explain.

The phenomenon I witnessed brought mixed emotions; will I see loved ones again? Will I safely retrace the steps I had taken over oceans and mountains that I took so long ago that brought me to this place? What is my future? The feelings running rampant in my mind brought anguish and vulnerability to strange forces tugging at my thoughts.

But the exuberance of youth prevailed and my somber mood passed. I went to the mess hall and ate my meal with gusto.

Today, I am scheduled to censor mail and that will keep my mind off morbid thoughts.

Tomorrow will bring other activities.

I may be scheduled for a bombing mission over Burma.

If not, there is always the countryside to be explored. The late afternoon may find me playing softball with the guys. And so the days pass—a few days closer to getting back home and assignment to safe stateside duty.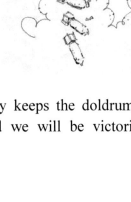

Some memories will fade only to be resurrected in future vivid reminiscences. I find that keeping busy keeps the doldrums at bay; the war will end eventually and we will be victorious. Amen.

NOISELESS BOMBS

From a height of 8,000 feet, the exploding bombs formed rosettes of varying hues as they impacted among, upon and near the railroad boxcars in central Burma. But what's this?? No booms, no satisfying sounds of rolling thunder I expected to hear?

This was my very first bombing mission and I was nervous, excited—and disappointed. When we bombardiers were in training in Midland, Texas, we were used to dropping training bombs which consisted of 95 pounds of sand and five pounds of black powder at altitudes of two to eight thousand feet. We were not surprised at not hearing any sounds of bomb impacts on targets, on the vast Texas plains.

But the movies and newsreels that we were exposed to convinced others and me that those war sounds were actual and not dubbed-in thunderous explosions.

Having had several "baptisms under fire," I felt like a real macho man and was not prepared for the various expressions used by some of the old-timers who were on the mission. "Milk run" was the expression most widely used by others after my first mission, which I considered a huge success. I was appalled; weren't we, after all, fired upon by anti-aircraft guns and then jumped by Zeros on our return trip to base? *If that was a milk run, what could I expect on real tough missions in the future?* I thought.

But, of course the "old pros" that had arrived some months before us and already had 30 to 40 combat missions under their belts were not easily rattled, and treated each bombing mission as just another duty to perform. It wasn't too long before we were

the hardened vets and looked up to by the most recent arrivals from the training bases in the States.

But this, my first mission, also provided memories that have stuck in my mind all these years. The Zero that jumped my plane with its green-as-grass crew reacted with the typical naiveté with which most American boys at first viewed our thrust into the serious business of fighting a war. So it was that that particular enemy plane which welcomed us to Burma was innocently viewed by us as an American "training" plane. But that is another story.

Bursting with the news of my first mission and just having to tell someone about it after de-briefing, I hotfooted it to my hut and immediately proceeded to put my impressions in a letter to my girl. I did not reckon on the heartlessness of the military censor. It was over four years later that I found out that the letter was delivered and the only things that were left of it after censoring was "Dear Frankie" and my signature at the bottom with the word "love" left intact. Boy oh boy, they sure knew how to destroy the heroics of a real life "red-blooded American hero!!!!!"

MONSOON

Monsoon—the very word struck terror in the heart of the seven year old boy daydreaming over his geography book, with its pictures of faraway places and events. The picture of a rickshaw pulled by a pigtailed coolie epitomized China. The lion conjured up vistas of African plains, while the monsoon, that rampaging outlaw of nature, symbolized India.

A hard rap with a ruler across my knuckles by a stern-faced nun brought me back to the reality of the complexities of subtraction, multiplication and addition—nowhere near as exciting as "mind travel" through time and space.

And now, almost seventeen years later, I found myself high up in the sky speeding eastward toward Burma in a war plane armed with deadly weapons and lethal bombs, skirting tremendous high-flying clouds that buffeted our planes with powerful winds, tremendous up and down drafts and thunderous rains. As I bounced around in my "greenhouse" area in the nose of the B-25, I found myself talking to no one in particular, asking myself over and over again, "What in Hell am I doing here, half a world away from home and in imminent danger of literally drowning, a mile and a half above the Bay of Bengal?"

With our plane gyrating crazily, I thought it was wise to leave my uncomfortable spot up front and crawl back to the navigator's compartment where the escape hatch in the floor was located. It was foolish reasoning, as jumping from the plane into the sea would be like "going from the frying pan into the fire." The pilot (name forgotten) was sweating bullets as he fought the controls in a world gone mad—tumbled gyros added to the turmoil. After a while, we broke through a small clearing in the clouds and dropped our bombs on some town we couldn't identify and simply recorded it as a "target of opportunity."

Once again we were engulfed by clouds, tops of which I estimated to be 35,000 to 40,000 feet. We fought the clouds again on return to base. I suppose the enemy thought that even those "crazy Americans" would not fly bombing missions in such adverse weather, as we did not encounter enemy resistance of any type.

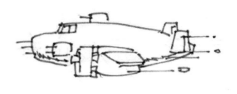

Upon return to our air base and safety, we assured the intelligence officer that the mission was a milk run. The resiliency of America's youth was proven yet again.

DEAD RECKONING NAVIGATION

After another foray into Burma with the monsoon still raging, we bombed our target and were on our way home to Chakulia, still evading huge clouds with gusts of rain spattering the windshield. We experienced the usual "elevator ride," up and down drafts with sickening regularity. After hitting our target (seen momentarily through a break in the clouds), we turned homeward. I had made just one drift run.

The skies cleared somewhat after passing Calcutta far off to the right, but still much of the terrain was obliterated by low-lying clouds. When we reached our ETA (estimated time of arrival), Elmer Thompson got on the intercom and asked me, "Where's the base?"

I answered, "Under that cloud." So we executed a 360 degree turn, all the while losing altitude and "voila!" there was our landing strip.

I suppose Elmer could have gotten a radio fix but he trusted me and flew according to my directions. All the crews learned to trust each other while training back in the States.

Training as a team and later fighting as a team really paid off when the "chips" were down.

WAR AND RUMORS

As happens everywhere in the world, rumors and tall tales abounding in war zones are spread. One of the many stories making the rounds concerned the Salween River bordering China and Burma. Whenever we managed to scrounge an Indian newspaper printed in English, we read it avidly from front to back, and that even included reading advertisements promoting the sale of various Indian consumer goods.

Native whiskeys were advertised under impossible names—particularly one brandy label which featured a picture of a tiger; we dubbed it "Panther Sweat." However, Canadian Very Special Reserve could be obtained in Calcutta at one place that operated under the logo "Peg Leg Pete's." Evidently, the Japanese soldiers preferred Canadian Rye to their native sake and would go to any length to obtain it, so the story goes. A front page tale would headline, "Chinese and Japanese forces skirmish at the Salween River," and it would go on to relate that the good guys won—routed the bad guys (Japanese). But rumor had it that, prior to any belligerent action, a truce would be called by both sides and there would be a lively exchange of goods between the combatants.

After mutually-satisfying trade negotiations were concluded, each side would retreat to its own lines, all the while firing their weapons into the air. After some time when certain goods were needed again, the charade would be repeated.

After each encounter, Calcutta's newspapers would then dutifully report enemy action at the Salween River. Of course the reports were always favorable and convinced us that we (allies) were kicking butt while never suffering any casualties in these successful activities.

Rumor, anyone?

A TRIBUTE TO FRED M. SIBLEY

After many years, events, places and individuals tend to dim in one's memory. Now and then a name pops up and the floodgates of memory open up and gush forth with long forgotten events and activities.

The name of Capt. Fred Sibley accomplished just that. He  briefed us on many missions, ably assisted by Major Arther. Here is a short version of one of my missions that was briefed by Capt. Sibley. I think he was a reservist who did his job well. I found him courteous, knowledgeable and every inch an officer. He was a credit to the service.

In early 1943, we were a seven-plane formation flying at 8,000 feet and were just passing Mt. Victoria when 2,000 feet below us a six-plane formation of Mitsubishi bombers, accompanied by Zero's, flew by heading west. I think they were on their way to hit either Chittagong or Calcutta and did not challenge us as we headed east to Mandalay.

The scuttlebutt was that we alerted the RAF and they gave the enemy a hot reception.

Just as we turned on to the bomb run, I got on the intercom and asked Elmer Thompson to go into a holding pattern—that old devil the "GI's" got me. I had to scramble to the rear of the plane to get to the chemical toilet. I was the lead bombardier of the formation and Elmer did not want to waste any time. The ack-ack was thick; the flashes and black smoke were getting closer.

Elmer was exasperated because I told him to follow the PDI (Pilot Direction Indicator used with the Norden bomb sight). Then, I got the hiccups and with each spasm the needle jiggled; he wound up making violent corrections trying to follow my directions. After a short session I got back on the Norden and made the bomb run—I held my breath in order to stifle the hiccups while putting the data into the bomb sight. Elmer was able to make a smooth run and we all hit the docks and warehouses at Mandalay, pretty much on target.

Later on we heard that we had also demolished the Japanese Officers' "House of Joy," which brought on many ribald tales that I will not repeat.

Well, our tales to Sibley at the de-briefing were later corroborated by aerial photographs.

YOU'LL LIKE IT FINE

When I drew officer of the day in Chakulia in early 1943, it was a memorable event. Accompanied by an MP Sergeant and a Jeep driver, we proceeded to drive around the perimeter of the base. We saw places I didn't know existed.

We checked out a warehouse type of building and, when I opened the door, I got the shock of my life. The place was stacked with coffins of varying hues, from floor to ceiling. We hurriedly pulled the door shut and hot-footed out.

This was written on the spur of the moment in 1943, in India, after listening to crewmen extolling the virtues of the B-25 Mitchell bomber, but with the haunting memories of those stacks of coffins still in my mind:

Thirty-five hundred horses pulling together
Through all kinds of foul weather;
Wings the shape of a gull,
A squat and sturdy hull.

Guns and cannon firing true,
Quarter ton bombs aloft in the blue,
Free as a bird, five times as fast,
(Was that a bullet we just passed?)

Oh, you'll like it fine, you'll like it fine.
(Don't think of that box made of pine.)

Thundering thru night, roaring thru day.
(Thank the lieutenant for flying pay.)
That's a real heavy engine when it's at rest,
At rest, at rest upon your chest.

Breakfast in Calcutta, lunch in Bombay,
Now honestly, wouldn't you like it that way?
I knew a hot-rock, a real old man,
Twenty five years was his life span.

Oh, you'll like it fine, you'll like it fine.
(Stop thinking of that box made of pine.)

She's fast and she's sleek, a real proud beauty.
Hard to handle, she's tricky but pretty;
The faster you go, the harder you hit,
(Pick me up gently, brother, bit by bit;)

Mac was a good pilot, he was really fine.
Next month he would have been twenty nine.
Climb? Two thousand feet a minute,
Man, she's fast as a bullet.

Oh, you'll like it fine, you'll like it fine.
(Why do I dream of a box made of pine?)

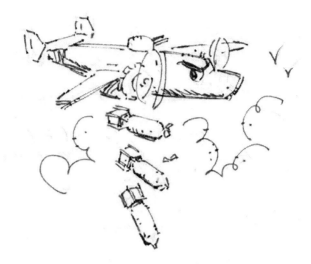

VOLUNTEER MISSION

"July 14—Bombed and strafed river shipping on Irrawaddy. Shwebo airport strafed and bombed from minimum altitude. Three large buildings blown up. Ground fire encountered was small arms and 20 mm cannon at point blank range."

The above was unearthed from my so-called diary, and at first sight gives no inkling to the thrills, and laughs, encountered on that mission. Let me describe the setting, the time and weather leading up to this mission.

It is July 14, 1943, at the Flying Eagle squadron's base in India. We had been busily bombing the Jap installations in north and central Burma, ranging from Myitkyina, Lashio, upper Salween and Mandalay down to Meiktila, Akyab and the Yenangyaung oil fields. Our principal targets were railroads, bridges, airfields and storage dumps. I had joined the squadron just three months before and had 20 missions under my belt. The monsoon weather had set in, making life miserable for everyone.

On this particular day, I lay in a sort of stupor on my bunk. Lying there lazily, thinking of nothing at all, I absently scratched myself trying to relieve a hellish heat rash. It had rained the night before, but the sun was out and it was blistering hot. The barrack I occupied was a mud hut; the walls were made of mud, kept in place by bamboo logs. The roof was a thick matting of rice straw, and the ceiling was whitewashed potato sacking stretched taught from wall to wall. The floor was a mixture of cement and mud, and it extended out about four feet from the building. An overhang of rice straws on bamboo supports created a porch-like affair. It lacked a half hour till noon.

On the porch I could hear desultory conversation. Two pilots stripped to the waist and perspiring profusely were making an attempt at playing cribbage. The barrack area was absolutely devoid of any other signs of life, except for a few stray bullocks, the buzzing of flies and probably a mangy dog or two looking for shade. The whole gave an appearance of listlessness, brought on by the oppressive heat. My Indian boy, whose name was Jacob Vadimonikum, but who was rechristened "Vade," stood in the doorway, balanced on one foot, not trying very hard to keep

awake. The peace and quiet was suddenly broken by a voice, yelling for "Stankiewicz!!!" I recognized the voice. It was Woody Campbell, a pilot with whom I've flown several missions. Woody was a California boy, a pink-cheeked, plump and cheerful ball of fire. I swear I never saw him anything but cheerful and smiling, even when the going was tough. Evidently, he spied Vade, because he said, "Hey, Bearer, where is Stankiewicz?"

Vade roused himself sufficiently to say, "He no here, Sahib."

"Well, who is in there?"

"Lootenint Shteve, Sahib."

"Then go in and tell him I want him."

A black head popped through the doorway and said, "Lootenint Shteve, fat man want you." At that, the two men outside playing cards broke out in guffaws, and brought a smile to my face, but Woody didn't take kindly to the description of himself.

I got up, and slipping my feet into a pair of GI shoes I stepped out, blinking my eyes in the dazzling sunshine. "What do you want, Woody?"

He replied, "Say boy, how'd ya like to go on a mission this afternoon? It's a volunteer mission. I hear it's a low level job."

"Volunteer?!!? ME?!!?? Ya nuts? You got rocks in your head? Nothin' doin'—I'm not volunteering for anything."

He came back, "Aw come on. It'll be fun. It's going to be a four-ship formation, and we're gonna go in on the deck. Just think of the time you'll have, shootin' up the countryside."

"Where's it to?" I asked cautiously, still not convinced that it would be a good idea to go against that old Army axiom, "Don't volunteer for anything."

"I don't know," Woody answered, "but briefing will be in a half hour at the S-2 office. Sibley will tell us all about it."

"Well, okay, I'll see you there."

"Swell—bring all your equipment and don't forget your escape kit."

Twenty minutes later he found me, with members of four other crews, sitting in the S-2 office. Lt. Sibley, our intelligence officer, walked in and immediately went into detail concerning the mission. On the wall in back of him was a map of central Burma. It was pockmarked with all sorts of symbols denoting enemy airfields, ack-ack positions, troop concentrations, etc.

As nearly as I can remember, here is the rough text of Sibley's talk. "Fellows, the Japs are getting troops and supplies to northern Burma, despite the damage we're doing to their railroads and bridges. Evidently, they're forcing the Burmese to repair the rails and bridges as quickly as we wreck them. We've got to put a more effective stop in their movements. As you know, we wrecked a lot of their rolling stock and they are acutely short of locomotives. If we can knock out more of them, we'll seriously hamper their movements for some time. Now—they have a lot of locomotives under repair in the Maymyo yards. Your job is to go in there and drop 500 ponders into the shops. That's why we want you to go in on the deck. The idea is to skip the bombs into the buildings, not through the tops of them. Now, here's the setup. The target area forms a rough horseshoe. You're to go into the open end of the shoe. You'll encounter machine gun fire from the tops of the buildings, on either side of you and directly in front of you."

Just then my heart deserted its normal place and fluttered down into my stomach. Sibley continued, "After you dump your bombs, you'll have to pull up steeply and chandelle to the right, because there will be high hills directly ahead. At this point, you'll be directly over the enemy barracks area and will probably get some small arms fire."

At the mention of this, my heart sank down, down, until I could feel it thumping in my shoes. He went on, "By the time you get to 1,000 feet you should have completed a 180 degree turn. You will now be over the polo field, and we believe that the Japs have several batteries of medium anti-aircraft fire there. But don't worry about it. They're pretty bum shots."

With this, he gave a little chuckle, but as I laughed hollowly along with him, I was bitterly cursing myself, "You dope, you sap, why can't you learn to keep your big fat mouth shut? Volunteer—huh!!!"

But the briefing wasn't over yet, not by a long shot. Sibley continued, "We believe that the Japs moved up a few fighters from Rangoon, but they're at Meiktila, about 100 miles south of Maymyo. So you won't have to worry about them—unless, of course, you alert them on the way to the target. Oh, yes, you know about Monywa, Sagaing and Mandalay; give those places a wide berth. Every one of those places has a bunch of ack-ack and they shoot pretty straight. And, keep away from the Shwebo airfield, because they might have a few fighters there. Well, that's about all, fellows. It shouldn't be too tough. You may run into some bad weather, and if you can't get into the target, pick a target of opportunity. The only thing that should keep you from your target is the weather. Any questions?"

QUESTIONS?!!? Hell no!! This will be duck soup. Oh yeah!!!

"Well, let's go, boy." Woody came up behind me, a grin from ear to ear on his face, and gave me a hearty thump on my back. The grin I gave him, I know, was sickly at best.

"You betcha, Woody, we'll give 'em hell."

We climbed aboard a truck, 24 strong, and headed for the revetments. During the short ride, I spend the time in somber musing. Six hundred miles, three hundred of it in enemy territory, in a four-ship formation without fighter escort didn't exactly stack up to a "milk run." But the mood quickly passed. The other boys were joking, laughing, and passing ribald remarks. As we stopped at each plane, the crew assigned to it hopped off and their gear was thrown out after them. "Get one for me," "So long, sucker," "Are they over that way? Okay, I'll go this way," we'd yell at their retreating backs as we roared off to our respective

ships. We quickly bombed up, checked our guns, and the pilots
pre-flighted the ships. We taxied
out to the strip and then, one by
one, we thundered down the
runway and were airborne.

After joining up with the
other ships, we set a course for
Maymyo. Calcutta, Bay of
Bengal, Chittagong and the Chin Hills passed under our wings,
and we were in Burma. There was no turning back now–come
what may, we were going to do our best to get through to our
objective and destroy it.

We were now at 10,000 feet, with the Chin Hills a couple of
thousand feet below. Looking far ahead, I spied the Chinwin
River. But that was as far as I could see, for beyond it was a
seemingly impenetrable wall of clouds. They reached up 35,000
feet in massive, tumbling disorder. We weaved in and out of
tumbling pillars; below us was a white sea of clouds, above us
only intermittent openings revealing a blue sky. And all the time
we were bumping along, as if riding a giant roller coaster in the
sky.

When we got to where Maymyo should be, we didn't dare let
down through the clouds for fear of crashing into the hills
surrounding it. Retracing our route, we began to let down
northeast of Sagaing, about 30 miles east of the legendary
Irrawaddy River. One by one, the other ships peeled off, winging
away to bomb other targets. We later learned that one of them hit
the ferry ships at Mandalay, and the other hit the City of
Paukkan. We decided to try to get into the primary target.

As we were skirting Mandalay, we noticed that we were not
alone. The fourth ship of our formation tagged along. But it was
absolutely impossible to get into Maymyo—the clouds were
hugging the ground tenaciously; visibility was nil.

Woody called up on the intercom and said that we'd go up the Irrawaddy and see what we could scare up. That was the beginning of the wildest plane ride that I ever had, or ever hope to have. The pilot shoved the throttles forward and we went roaring up the river, indicating 250 MPH. The shore line was just a blur. But anything that floated in that river wasn't safe from our guns. Carefully concealed river junks, boats and sampans come into view. Every gun on our ship opened up and the noise was deafening.

It really was a field day for all of us. As our bullets walked up and into the boats, tiny brown figures hurtled out and dove into the water. The four fixed guns fired by the pilot kept up an incessant chatter and the smoke and smell of powder filled my compartment.

After having shot up at least a dozen boats we turned off the river and headed westerly. We came upon a railroad and followed it south. Camouflaged locomotives and railroad cars on sidings flashed by beneath us and we poured hundreds of rounds of tracer, armor-piercing and incendiary bullets into them, and the gunners howling like Comanches. On a siding, just south of Pintha, we came upon a score of box cars. We were so low I could see the paint peeling on the <u>sides</u> of the cars—dirty yellows and reds and greens. All I had to do was tick out the bombs without sighting.

I dropped my first bomb fixed with an eleven second delay fuse. It hit in the center of a string of cars. We climbed a couple of hundred feet and turned, and an unusual sight hit our eyes. When the bomb hit it tumbled three cars completely off the tracks, without exploding!!! But even as we looked goggle-eyed, the bomb exploded. The earth seemed to erupt and pieces of the cars flew high in the air.

Looking out to the side, we saw our other ship making a run on a large building; all of its guns were blazing. That was the last I saw of that plane until we got back to the home base.

We kept on and roared over Shwebo airfield—the place we were to avoid if we could help it. As the empty revetments flashed by under us, I saw a Jap cantonment on the left, and several hundred yards ahead was a two-story building housing the control tower. I aimed my 30 caliber machine gun with my left hand and poured an even 100 rounds into the Jap tents, meanwhile sighting and firing a .50 caliber with my right hand at the building straight ahead.

As we neared the building, I let lose my grip on the .30 caliber gun and opened the bomb bay. The big gun jammed at that moment and I had no time to get it to fire. Scrambling around a 20 mm cannon in a window of a building were several Japs. Just as they trained the gun on us, I screamed to the pilot, "Shoot,

shoot, my gun's jammed!!!" The pilot punched the button and his four fifties cut down the Jap gunners. I released two bombs and the pilot pulled up steeply, missing the top of the building by inches. We went about 200 feet and turned to the right. We completed a 180 degree turn just in time to see the building and those sons of Nippon go flying skyward.

Still in the grip of excitement, yelling and ranting, we tore on to another target. Two buildings loomed ahead; from their size we figured them to be warehouses.

Firing as we went, I ticked out two more bombs, and again we performed the same maneuver—up and around. And again the same satisfying sight—pieces of the building flying skyward. The pieces seemed to float up lazily, hung momentarily several hundred feet above the ground and then plunged earthward, scattering in all directions.

With our bombs expended and almost all of our ammunition shot up, it was time to go home. The pilot cautioned us to conserve what was left of our ammunition and we winged homeward, happy but tired.

One of the gunners with us was S/Sgt. Oscar Smith, an irrepressible little screwball, and he loved firing his guns. We were still buzzing along a few feet above the ground, and the sight of occasional targets was more than he could stand.

Shortly after the cease fire order was given, there sounded a short "brrrrp" from the rear. Woody yelled over the intercom, "Cut it out, we want to have some ammo left in case we run into some fighters."

All was quiet for several minutes when, "brrrp," it came again. Woody got a little peeved. "Boy, if I hear so much as a peep out of those guns, you'll be digging slit trenches for a week."

A meek, "Yessir," came back.

"Aw, Woody," I interposed, "take it easy on the guy."

"Quiet, bombardier, or you'll be digging one, too."

I answered with a gulp. But knowing Woody as we did, we knew he was laughing to himself. He just wasn't built to be rough on anybody.

Presently, we began our climb until we reached the necessary altitude to clear Chin Hills. As we crossed the last chain of mountains, the tension was broken. We were out of enemy territory and a feeling of relief flowed through.

Woody, as usual, got on the intercom singing, interspersing song with occasional, "Boy, we sure gave them hell, didn't we?" and, "So solly, Cholly," and so forth. He sure loved to crow over each successful mission. Everybody got a verbal pat on the back as his expansiveness grew.

Just as we expected, the first thing he said when we landed was, "Look, you guys, I didn't mean to yell at you—but heck, we didn't want to shoot up all of our ammunition, did we?"

We, of course, feigned indignation. We heckled him until he threw up his hands and stomped off. The mission was over. The only thing left now was to report to S-2 for interrogation. The reaction set in and as we gathered up our gear a weakness crept over us.

And here is what I remember most about this mission. Before we left the plane, a Jeep drove up and the armament officer got out. He looked into the plane and when he saw the empty cartridges scattered all over the floor, he gave a long whistle. Trying hard to look stern and unsuccessfully hiding a grin, he growled, "What's the idea of shooting up all the ammunition? Don't you know it's a hard job loading all those guns?"

THE ENEMY ... SO CLOSE ... 1943

A high level bombing mission, for the most part, is impersonal and detached. The only sign of enemy activity below is the ack-ack that appears silently and malevolently, red flashes within black explosive clouds in and around our formation of medium bombers. But low-level attacks bring the war and its increased dangers up close and extremely personal.

One of my low-level missions was the mining of the Irrawaddy River. In between monsoon rains I was in one plane of a small formation scheduled for this activity. As I recall the occasion, the mines were supplied by the British.

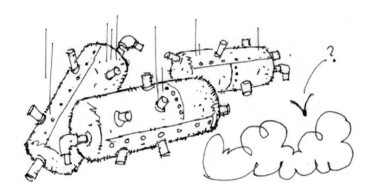

The 1000 pound mines were cylindrical things looking much like galvanized hot water tanks. Each plane carried three of those monstrosities. The fuses were supplied by the British and they instructed us on how to arm them. Special bomb shackles were devised by our own men. The plan implemented was for each plane to drop the mines at specified distances. Supposedly, the action of the river water would arm the mines at intervals of one to three days and the passage of enemy supply boats would set them off.

After dropping our mines, we were on our own. My plane crew took this as carte blanche to shoot up the countryside. As we flashed by, over junks and sampans, some hidden in the brush along the shore, we gave them quick bursts of .50 caliber machine gun fire. We also concentrated on river traffic and observed the crews jumping overboard for their lives.

But my most vivid memory was seeing a Japanese officer coming out of a riverside hut, hands on hips, looking up at us nonchalantly as we roared by at tree top level. We were so low that I distinctly saw the "spit shine" on his black shoes and razor sharp crease on his khaki pants. The whole object of our operation was to prevent supplies from reaching enemy forces at the Salween River. Hopefully we kept the enemy from enjoying rice balls and fish heads for a few days.

Ah! Such is war!

TRUST

On one of my bombing missions we were returning to base and were already over friendly territory. As lead bombardier/navigator it was my duty to know our exact location at all times; the rest of the formation simply followed and sometimes didn't bother keeping track of location or compass heading if they did not feel like doing so.

It was no surprise when one of our wingmen called in the clear, "Elmer, I'm having engine trouble. How do I get to Dum Dum airport?" Elmer Thompson, my pilot, got on intercom and asked me if I could help.

I awoke from my reverie in my greenhouse up front and did some swift calculations to verify our location. "Elmer, tell him to make a ninety degree turn to the right. It should put him on exact course to Dum Dum," I said.

Unquestioningly, the wingman peeled off and soared away.

It would serve no useful purpose to name the crew of that "lost pigeon"—it could happen to anyone; navigating in that area of the world was difficult; we had to concern ourselves with plains, deltas, mountains, the Bay of Bengal and monsoons a lot of the time. In time, we lead navigators began to recognize hills, rivers and other identifying marks to aid us in getting to our targets and then back home to our air base. My favorite landmark was Mount Victoria and I was always glad to see her white-capped mountaintop whenever my route took me past "Her Royal Highness."

The purpose of this little tale is to show how much confidence crews had in one another. We relied on each other's abilities and every bombing mission was a team effort.

SOBERING THOUGHTS ABOUT CALCUTTA

After a half century I am still uncomfortable by some recollections of the seamy side of life in that Asian land. This short thumbnail sketch may revive mixed emotions in the hearts of you readers.

As I gazed out the window of my room overlooking a rooftop extension of the Grand Hotel one early morning, I was struck with the incongruity of it all; whereas back home under similar circumstances, one would be treated to the sight of a pigeon roosting on roof tops and window ledges, here in India the roofs were filled with solemn-looking buzzards, harbingers of death and decay.

The streets below were already filled with taxis, bullock carts, free-roaming cattle and gharry-wallahs heartlessly whipping their emaciated horses to greater efforts. The poor hungry beasts could only manage a half-hearted trot at best. The throngs of coolies dragging their passengers in rickshaws amidst the pedestrian mob of humanity added to the din and horrendous disorder.

And marching behind the cattle and horse-drawn gharrys were the poor disenfranchised and most unhappy of all, the untouchables, listlessly gathering up the animal excrement so abundantly contributed by the sacred bovines in the streets. The sacred cows of India were all over, on sidewalks, on the roads, blocking doorways and getting in the way of people and traffic in general.

"Mother India"—the short phrase flitted through my mind—the mother of motley humanity, displaying a cleavage of startling differences; on the one hand the rich and arrogant Brahmins and on the other the dirt poor remnants of a huge nation of unhappy souls the world seemed to have forgotten—those that appeared to have emerged from a vacuum and face a vacuum in the hopeless future.

And amidst all this cacophony of sound and movement were the ubiquitous beggars, ranging in age from mere toddlers to snaggle-toothed old men and women almost all on the verge of starvation, bodies covered with lesions and sores with hurt and hopelessness

 mirrored in their expressive eyes. And—we strangers from a far off land barely noticing the emptiness of the present and future of this unhappy place.

Our early individual efforts to alleviate the suffering of at least a few poor souls were discouraged, first by the advice of long-term inhabitants from around the globe and secondly, by our final realization of the enormity of the problem that beset that struggling nation. For, even as we temporary military visitors finally came to terms with ourselves, we could not honestly salve our conscience, and all that we observed and felt never ceased to haunt us. Bitter memories!

FAMINE, STARVATION
AND DEATH

One day on a three-day pass I visited Calcutta, during the famine of 1943. I was aghast at what I saw in the streets of that huge Asian metropolis. The stench of death was overpowering. In the narrow byways of the city the poor homeless vagabonds lay where they fell, victims of starvation and pestilence.

It was so bad that the British government sent a Viceroy to take some action that would alleviate the suffering of the hungry and take steps to prevent a deadly plague that was sure to come if conditions there were ignored. The first step was to clear the streets of the dead and to dispose of them in a manner most suitable to solve the problem.

Feeding the hungry was another matter. I walked the streets of Calcutta and saw emaciated human bodies lying in the streets and doorways of rickety homes. Some of the poor suffering people were on the verge of death and many were already out of their misery. I observed natives pushing two-wheeled carts containing dead bodies. I saw two men at each cart stopping at each supine body, kick them and those that moved were left alone. But those that did not respond to the kick were presumed

dead and were unceremoniously picked up and thrown onto the cart as just so much cordwood.

This procedure was followed as the two men progressed down the street. When full up they wheeled their grisly charge to I knew not where.

But I, as inquisitive as ever, asked one team what they did with the bodies.

I was informed that each load was thrown on huge fires at the edge of the river ghats (ceremonial steps).

This procedure was followed until the streets were clear of the dead and the danger of plague was past. I believe that something like 30,000 people died each week in Calcutta alone in that year of 1943. The government reversed the trend by supplying foodstuffs and medications for those fortunate enough to have survived the famine.

From the steps of the Grand Hotel, black clouds of smoke could be seen in the distance, which I assumed were from the fires at the ghats. It was also safe to assume that the stench of burning bodies was overpowering.

I have always honored and appreciated our country and these horrific happenings only serve to stiffen my back and, more than ever, convince me that all I stood for was worth fighting for.

GOD BLESS AMERICA.

BAT BOYS

When not on a bombing mission or not having some duty to perform, some of us managed to amuse ourselves in various ways. To help pass the time, we played softball, touch football and the game of monopoly. Pinochle, cribbage and poker helped fill in empty moments. And some fellows who, having had some contact with British officers, tried to emulate their "savoir faire."

Carrying a riding crop was considered to be "derigueur" and having a "bat boy" was a must. Bat boys are persons who are not quite valets but are those who ran errands, did the laundry, polished shoes, etc.; in other words, "gofers."

Early on, Mike Russell and I hired a bearer to do just those things but we did not call him "bat boy." He was just a bearer to us.

Our bearer was a lad of thirteen or so who had a name that was unpronounceable. He had a perpetual smile, exposing buck teeth, so we called him "buckshot."

He was slightly built, with the biggest feet imaginable. At times, Mike and I were at a loss as to how to keep him gainfully employed, with the result that Buckshot had plenty of time off. But he tried to teach us rudimentary Hindustani and we picked up many native expressions.

Mysteriously, he disappeared for days at a time, particularly when our clothes were in need of washing. But one day he disappeared for good.

In the past when he went AWOL he eventually returned but we could not get any information out of him as to where he went, what he did, if he was sick or whatever. He just grinned and went out looking busy.

The day he disappeared for good was the day everyone lined up at the dispensary for shots. Buckshot was curious as to what was happening. Truthfully, I didn't know what the heck the shots were for either but dutifully lined up as everyone else did. (Probably a "desert shot.")

Jokingly, we urged Buckshot to get the shot along with us. It took a bit of coaxing but finally we convinced him that the inoculation would do him good and prevent him from getting sick. We watched one man after another get the shot and move on. Buckshot found himself behind a guy we knew to be a perpetual clown who, when jabbed with a needle, let out a yell and fell to the ground with a frightful groan.

Buckshot, seeing this, his eyes as big as saucers, whooped and took off at top speed never to be seen again.

So—Jakob Vademonikum entered out lives. We named him Vade.

Vade was about thirty years of age, very quiet, sober and reserved. He washed our khakis regularly and the constant beating they took on wash day frayed them in short order. The laundry room was a flat rock on a stream upon which Vade laid the clothes, soaped them up and pounded the articles with a stick. He then rinsed them in the stream. When dried in the hot sun, the shirts and pants were as stiff as boards.

Well, Vade was with us for quite a spell. In time he sent for his wife and children and brought them to a nearby village where they lived for months. Vade kept the usual work hours with Saturdays and Sundays off.

Unbeknownst to us, Vade had a goal in mind. More about that shortly.

A couple of months after our arrival in Chakulia, packages from home began to arrive. I'm sure our donors didn't get together to decide on what articles to send to us but the sameness of the items was astounding: toothpaste, shaving cream, toothpaste, shaving cream, toothpaste, shaving cream and more shaving cream. In time I had enough toothpaste to last for years so I gave some to Vade (the Spam he wouldn't take).

Toothpaste was unknown to rural India but they had a handy substitute which was a twig from a certain tree. I observed natives scrubbing their teeth with such twigs, which created a foam-like toothpaste.

One day, I asked Vade how he liked the Colgates, Pepsodent, etc., that I gave him and he answered "Goot, Sahib. Goot for vash face, vash hands, vash feet—very goot, Sahib." I didn't care as long as he didn't eat the stuff.

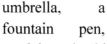

Vade did some moonlighting on the side and accumulated enough rupees to realize hope of all ambitious Indians—he purchased an umbrella, a fountain pen,

sandals and a bicycle. He was now a man of means. One day he came to Mike and me to announce his resignation and was now all set to gather his family and head for the big city. He was mission-educated and I'm sure obtained a job as a pencil pusher in some cubby-hole office where he happily attained his dream. India—ah India—ah, memories.

HOIMAN—THE SHREW
THAT WENT TO WAR

He died a heroic death. There were no ceremonies, no muffled drums and no flag-draped caisson to give him an appropriate sendoff. Nevertheless, he was sorely missed by two of Uncle Sam's fighting men. You see, Hoiman died in the field of action. He died in the line of duty.

Perhaps, here, I should fill in his background. During the Burma campaign, I was stationed in the Province of Bengal, fighting off the onslaughts of every imaginable type of insect known (and unknown) to man, in addition to fighting the enemy in my role as bombardier. My humble abode was a straw-roofed mud hut. My ten by ten foot room contained two beds, two foot lockers, two wooden crates and two rough planks. The planks, stretched across the crates, made a fairly good writing table. Of windows and doors there were none. My roommate was a slow, easy going Air Force officer by the name of Ellsworth Valentine, Val for short.

Night falls swiftly and completely in India. Our source of illumination was a kerosene lantern. By its friendly light, Val and I wrote many a homesick letter home. It also lent its rays in aiding us to keep a close check on each other to see that there was no cheating as we silently played solitaire. I stopped counting my games after I reached the 2,999th game.

Our routine seldom varied. After the evening meal, we would wash and return to our room. The Indian night rushed over us and then the lantern would be hung up and lit. A couple of hours were spent, either in writing letters or in playing solitaire. Finally, the light would be extinguished and Val and I would crawl into our hot, uncomfortable cots, tuck in the mosquito netting and then spend an interminable time furiously courting Morpheus. But the lantern was also a source of inconvenience to us. When its beneficent rays lit up our room it sent out an irresistible invitation to all the walking, crawling, flying insets of all of India into our room. They buzzed, ticked, chirped, jumped—and they all bit. Whether playing cards or writing letters, each activity was interspersed with loud slaps and soft curses.

On one particularly hot and muggy evening, I was sitting at the table, attempting to compose a letter home. Val sat on his cot, methodically slapping at his torso and, with equal regularity, sipping a mixture of whiskey and lukewarm water. The latter activity undoubtedly prevented him from filling the air with sulfurous invective. In the middle of my writing, Val, in a conversational monotone, asked, "What is it?"

Never being one unable to keep up my end of a sparkling conversation I replied, "What's what?"

Val, after what seemed like a five minute interval answered, "That thing by your left big toe." I continued to write. After a lengthy interval, his remark penetrated my inner consciousness. When it did, I was galvanized into action. With a startled yelp I was off my stool and onto my cot in one bound. Val did all but roll on the floor in a paroxysm of laughter. Gads, but that man had iron control!! He didn't spill a drop of his horrible concoction as he howled and rooted in glee.

After my threatening to brain him with a shoe, he regained his ordinary restraint long enough to point out to me the reason for his question. In a dark corner, with his beady eyes flicking from Val and then to me, his tiny nose twitching, there sat IT. IT was a shrew. My first impulse was to quickly end its existence, but just then it performed a duty that spared its life and inducted it into the United States Army Air Force. Even while we were looking at it, a ponderous beetle winged into the room and, like a mighty buzzing dreadnought, flew blindly into the wall with an audible thump. The beetle bounced off and fell to the floor. In a flash, the shrew was upon it and, with dispatch, rid India of one of its insect inhabitants.

Val and I <u>shrewdly</u> analyzed the situation. Here in our midst was a fellow soldier, a comrade in arms. I went to my foot locker and removed a bottle from my precious hoard. (Val's eyes lit up in anticipation. Then his face took on a grim expression. I guess he would never have so willingly shared his bottle if he knew what I had in my footlocker. Naturally, I had completely forgotten I had a bottle or two cached away. It took a momentous occasion such as this to bring it to mind.) I opened the bottle and for the next half hour Val and I sipped whiskey and water, all the while discussing ways and means to induct the shrew into the Air Force.

It was a terrific problem because our new-found friend had no name. And how could you commission someone or something that had no name? Finally, it came to us in a flash. We decided to give the shrew the name Hoiman. Val, who by this time was just a wee bit unsteady, looked around until he spotted the shrew. Taking the bottle in hand, he raised it aloft saying, "I pronounce thee Hoiman." My quick intervention saved Hoiman from becoming a battleship, because the bottle was in its downward swing when I caught Val's arm. In the meantime, Hoiman's appearance had undergone a radical change. He had by this time gorged himself on all manner of insects and his little midriff was as round as a tennis ball.

Hoiman lived on with us for several months. His appetite was enormous. Each night, long after the light was put out and Val and I were in our cots, Hoiman scurried about in relentless pursuit of his enemies.

Val, having been in India longer than I, passed on some useful information to me. He knew that a shoe was an irresistible bed for scorpions. He cautioned me to shake out my shoes before putting them on in the mornings. One dark morning, I was awakened at four o'clock to go on a bombing mission. I reached for my shoes and shook them out. Something fell out with a thump. I reached under my pillow for the flashlight, feeling certain that if it were a scorpion it must be the granddaddy of all the scorpions in India. By the light of my flashlight I saw a thoroughly angry Hoiman. In the night, he evidently took over my shoe as his domicile.

He didn't take too kindly to his violent disturbance of slumber. Right then and there he transferred his allegiance from me to Val. With a baleful glance over his shoulder, Hoiman headed straight across the room and into Val's shoe. He popped out again to shrivel me with an indignant glance. With a last angry wiggle of his short tail, he retired for the night.

The months passed and our bombing of the enemy bases in Burma went on apace. At times, half of the combat personnel on our base would be out on a raid, and many times would stay overnight at a forward base in order to hit the enemy once again before returning home.

One night, I found myself the only one left behind in my area of the bunkhouses. Our base was laid out in a crescent and my hut was in the extreme outer edge of the crescent, with the jungle at my back door. After saying good night to Hoiman, I put out the light and lay down to sleep. But Hoiman's work was still far from over as he kept on industriously in his slaughter of insects. In the dead of the night I awoke with a strange feeling of premonition that all was not well. The night was deathly still. It must have been the unnatural stillness that awakened me, for ordinarily the jackals keep the night alive with their cacophony of sound while the hyenas add zest to it with their madman's laughter.

When I came fully awake, I realized that I was lying on my right side with my back to the room. I felt a chill run up my spine and the hairs on the back of my neck felt as if they were standing out stiffly. Something warned me that I was not alone, that there was something in the room. But whether it was man or beast, I did not know. Slowly I turned over, my eyes searching the inky darkness. After several minutes I distinguished a large shape at the foot of Val's cot. I strained my eyes, but couldn't make out what it was.

The only sound in the room was the panting of the thing sitting or standing there. Visions of man-eating tigers, ferocious baboons and what not crowded my brain. But whatever it was, I wasn't going to lie there and do nothing. I had my Colt .45 hanging in its holster by the cot, but it was on the outside of the mosquito netting. With infinite care I slowly inched my hand out under the netting and grasped the pistol. The movement of the THING halted my hand momentarily. But, when nothing further happened, I began extracting the pistol from the holster. Finally, I had it in hand. And then I moved quickly. I pulled back the barrel and let it fly. As it shot home it seated a cartridge in place, ready to fire. The clacking noise sounded as loud as thunder in the unnatural stillness, and sent the THING out the door like a streak.

I didn't have a chance for a shot. But whatever it was, it killed off all hope of sleep for me for the rest of the night.

I got out of bed and lit the lantern. With a shaking hand I struck a match and lit a cigarette. I sat and cudgeled my brain. What in the world could that thing have been? As my eyes roved around the room, I saw something that chilled my blood. There, stretched out in the doorway was Hoiman. He was dead. Hors de combat. Kaput. He lay on his side, a half-eaten beetle in his mouth.

Oh, I know what people will say. They'll say that Hoiman got up for an evening snack and wandered into the path of that fleeing thing, beast or devil, whatever it was, and was trampled to death, a victim of his gluttony. But I know better. I alone realize what happened. Hoiman awoke to find me, a buddy, in deadly peril, and with extreme courage and utter disregard for his own safety, ATTACKED. He drove it off and sent it scurrying, at the cost, alas, of his own life.

Hoiman, wherever you are, I want you to know that I shall never forget you. You will live in my heart forever. Your supreme sacrifice will not go unsung. Hoiman, I thank you. Hoiman, buddy, fellow soldier, I salute you.

WHAT—ME WORRY?

Upon arriving in India in 1943, my imagination ran riot, especially at an air base in Karachi, a place some of us stayed a day or two before continuing on to whatever destiny may befall us. The first day, as I was sitting in my room getting ready to catch a ten-wheeler into town, a jackal meandered into my room and without even so much as a glance at me, it sauntered out the other doorway, intent on some jackal business he had in mind. I, of course, was agape in wonder. Was it possible a hyena or even a tiger might use my room as a shortcut to whatever place it had in mind?

However, sight-seeing and a fine luncheon in Karachi soon dispelled my trepidation. The acrobats, snake charmers, magicians and jugglers performing in the streets won my attention. Thoughts of wild beasts flitted from my mind. As time passed, we gave no thought to the ever-present dangers of cobras as we stomped through fields and brush, totally unconcerned.

One example of this constant danger was the evening when a cobra invaded the nurses' quarters. A visitor dispatched the snake with a well-placed shot from his ever-present Colt 45.

QUITE A DAY AT CHAKULIA

I yawned mightily as I stretched, upon emerging from my room and onto the porch of my hut. I was not scheduled for a mission this day so I slept late and missed breakfast. As I gazed around sleepily, a truck full of Indian boys and girls singing loudly drove by, each one carrying either a shovel or a pick ax, on their way to areas on the base needing repair of washed out roads; all in all a happy group in contrast to my sober mood.

Some of the girls were slightly (?) pregnant. The heat of the day was already oppressive. Oh well, a shower and shave may make me feel better and the dark mood will pass.

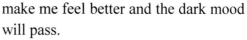

After cadging *(getting by begging)* some toast and coffee at the mess hall, I came fully awake, becoming cognizant of the world around me, such as noticing the dirt roads, the huts baking in a relentless sun and noticing a cur dog ambling along sniffing the ground. The sound of buzzing insects added to the listlessness of a depressing montage that was greeting another day bereft of human activity.

But wait—a cha wallah appears, vending his ware of tepid tea carried in a red clay pot perched atop his head. He looks hopefully at me, trying to make a sale. I flipped him a coin, an anna or a pice, but declined his proffered cup of tea.

Then my attention became riveted on the dog ambling along. It was totally unaware of an airman waving a Colt 45 and rapidly gaining on the scrawny mutt. Suddenly, the dog became aware of the guy chasing it. Looking backward, the dog ran blindly into a tree that was near my hut. The poor thing howled pitifully as his nemesis aimed the gun at him—and the poor creature was on its way to dog heaven.

"Why did you shoot the dog?" I asked the executioner.

"He raped my puppy," he shouted. It was useless to tell him that animals only did what came naturally and that was no cause for violent behavior on his part. But the guy was really steamed and still had his gun in hand so I kept my mouth shut and went inside my room until he left. I reasoned that is was most prudent to exercise discretion.

In time, some men (Indian natives) happened by and took the carcass away. (Probably someone's "filet mignon" that night.)

But wait—there was more excitement this day. As I came out onto the porch I sensed a flurry of activity in the crown of the nearby tree. There, high up, a drama was being played out. I spotted a raven relentlessly pursuing a lizard (chameleon?) who, time after time, wriggled from the beak of its pursuer. The raven was determined to have its lunch. Finally, the prey animal leaped down to the ground and dashed for the brush, hotly pursued by the hungry bird.

At mid-morning, one of the work crew, a young girl, came and laid a new-born babe on a shawl stretched out on the ground. She evidently gave birth while plying her pick ax on the road. And now, after dusting off sand and ants from her child, she left and returned to the work gang.

I was appalled and worried and wondered about the baby. At noon, the truck full of workers stopped by and the new mother gathered up her child. By this time the child was screeching lustily, probably noisily proclaiming to all and sundry that it was hungry and wanted to be fed post haste. As the young mother and babe rejoined the others on the truck, they all oohed and aahed over the latest addition to India's teeming millions. The truck drove off, its passengers singing loudly and happily. Life goes on.

THE WALDORF

There was a three or four-room thatched-roof building on our base at Chakulia, India, in 1943. It was used primarily as sleeping quarters for recruits or others passing through on their way to permanent assignments or as replacements for those old-timers who had achieved enough points to be rotated back to the States.

The replacements were greeted with open arms as I shall relate here. Let me say right up front that I had absolutely, positively, no part in this particular welcoming committee even though my luxurious (?) quarters were only a hop, skip and a jump from the Waldorf. I'm just relating this tale as I got it through the grapevine.

One night, a newcomer was billeted in the Waldorf; after stowing his gear the guy meandered over to the Officers Club for much needed refreshment, mainly gin and lime mixed with warm water, a potent concoction.

While he was occupied ingesting the drinks, some prankster led a cow into the victim's room and thoughtfully tethered it to the cot. He also put six or seven live chickens on the cot and secured the mosquito netting in place to ensure the fowl did not escape. Of course, the cow did what cows do when reacting to the call of nature. Meanwhile, the chickens went to sleep on the cot. Refrigeration was not a luxury we had in the mess hall, so the cook kept chickens alive and fresh in crates until they were ready for the pot.

Our "hero" found his room in the dark and walked into the rear of the cow and "polished" his shoes in the waste produced by said cow. Oh well, no big deal; he simply untied the cow, turned it around in the small space and led the bovine outside and sent it on its way with a pat on the rump. He then took off his shoes and socks and set them outside. He pulled back the netting for a much needed sleep. This woke up the chickens who took umbrage at being disturbed and with much squawking and clucking, feathers flying, they flew out the door and fled into the brush. (There went our Sunday dinner.)

The guy was now in a dangerous frame of mind. One can just imagine him standing barefoot in mellifluous excreta, waving his Colt 45 and screaming at the top of his lungs, "I'll kill the S.O.B. who did this— I'll kill him!"

I wish to stress again, I had no part in this prank. Even so, I gave this guy a wide berth until he was assigned elsewhere and I had no fear of running across him anytime soon.

The pithy observation by William Tecumseh Sherman, "War is Hell," is so true!

OH HAPPY DAY!

That day in 1943 when many of us received a liquor shipment became a memorable day. It was the first and only time we were able to get such a treat. Some of us got whiskey while others got cases of beer. I obtained a quart of Canadian VSR and a bottle of gin or vodka, I don't remember which.

As I was sitting in my room admiring my prize, Tony Mercep and several of his buddies came in with the object of trading—their beer for my whiskey. I was all for it as I preferred beer. Then in a spirit of camaraderie we decided to celebrate the trade by having a nip or two, washed down by cans of beer. One way or another, the whiskey and beer disappeared. Empties were scattered all over the room. Also, things were a little fuzzy.

Well, as chow time was approaching, Tony and his cohorts decided it was time to leave. They bid me farewell with much

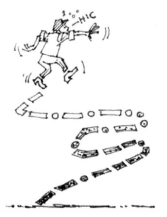

back-slapping and repeated assurances that I was the best goldarn pal that ever lived. I watched as they stumbled down the road with much weaving from side to side.

They must have traveled half a mile while advancing only fifty yards in a forward direction. At the rate they were going, it probably took them an hour to complete a five minute walk. Tony, the sober one, had his hands full trying to keep them going in the right direction. As for myself, I had no idea why I felt out of sorts. I decided to take a nap.

Upon awakening, I called Mike Russell next door and we went to the mess hall for dinner.

Just as we sat down, two sobriety-deprived pilots staggered in and joined us on our bench. In the center of the table was a large bowl of mashed potatoes, which I eyed hungrily. (We were served, mostly, country-style, hence the big bowl of spuds.) One of the tipsy guys pulled the bowl toward him and proceeded to eat from the bowl with the serving spoon. After a while, he stopped eating and nodded off—I watched, fascinated as his head drooped, and just before his nose hit the potatoes, he jerked upright and began eating from the bowl again. After two or three near misses, the inevitable happened—he went head first into the bowl of mashed potatoes and fell sound asleep.

He looked so comfortable I hated to wake him up. But then his buddy shook him awake and they stumbled out, one with mashed potatoes in his hair, nose and chin sporting dabs of white giving him the appearance of an old time Kentucky Colonel. I don't know why, but I lost interest in that bowl of mashed potatoes.

Meantime, the punkah wallahs sitting at each end of the room were tirelessly swinging the punkah which was suspended from the ceiling midway in the room. Hopefully, this activity would circulate the air and possibly cool off the room a smidgen. The punkah is a large wooden frame covered with burlap and is pulled back and forth, making it a primitive air conditioner. Also, the swinging of the punkah shook the ceiling and dislodged unwanted denizens nestled in the cracks and grooves, including a maggot or two now and then.

The dessert that night was chocolate pudding and we eagerly looked forward to satisfying our yearning for sweets. Mike had a spoonful half way to his mouth when a bug dropped from the ceiling and onto his spoon.

He moaned, "Ugh," and pushed away his dish. I may have been a bit finicky but the dessert did not look too appetizing to me any more.

Later in the evening, I played cards in the club house and on the way back to my hut, noticed a light in the back of the mess hall. I went over to look and saw the native cook kneading dough for the next day's meals. Attracted by the kerosene lantern, the air was full of flying insects and some unfortunate ones were being trapped in the dough in large numbers.

"Sonofagun," I thought to myself, "and all this time I thought I was eating raisin bread." From then on, I wouldn't eat bread unless it was toasted. "If you can't see it, it can't hurt you." Thus ended another interesting day in exotic Chakulia, India.

VAL AND THE MONKEY

My roomie, Ellsworth Valentine, was experiencing difficulty in breathing while asleep one night in our hut.

Unwisely, Val left packages of Wrigley's Spearmint and various other kinds of chewing gum on top of his footlocker. A monkey helped itself to Val's treasure trove of chewing gum and was chewing the gum and happily tearing off the wrappers, chewing and swallowing the gum while sitting on top of the mosquito netting. The monkey, whether somebody's pet or from the wild, caused his weight to sag the netting lower and lower until full weight rested on Val's chest. This wakened Val and he shouted and swatted the monk, which then quickly leaped off and scooted out the doorway (we had no doors).

I often thought about this animal, wondering if all that chewing gum effectively sealed off an important part of its lower anatomy.

POOL PARTY

The monsoon rains had stopped and suffocating heat enveloped all. Dry river beds were now raging torrents and stone bridges were under water. This was India at its worst.

Somehow, someone, (perhaps our commanding officer) arranged a pool party at the invitation of the Jones family who offered us the use of the pool at their private residence some distance away from our air base. Mr. Jones was an executive at the TATA Steel Works, one of the world's largest steel producers at that time.

Two ten-wheelers were dispatched bearing happy airmen, all looking forward to the unexpected treat. On the way we had to cross a couple of stone bridges which were inundated and could not be seen under the rushing waters.

A happy solution was to have a native stand on the front bumper and signal our driver which way to go to safely traverse the  treacherous route. The native knew the way to the Jones residence so he became our guide. (The powerful raging current would have to be faced again on the return trip, but— who cared?)

The way to our destination was mostly over dirt roads with a small village here and there drowsing in the sun. Signs along the way advertised various local products, such as salve that guaranteed to cure venereal disease, urging one and all to drink Tiger brand brandy, English made cigarettes and various unpalatable-looking Indian goodies.

Billboards advising "Yankee go home" were numerous, and disconcerting.

We arrived at the Jones home and were greeted by Mrs. Jones, with pitchers of iced lemonade.

The pool was large and inviting, soon filling with shouting, diving airmen splashing around merrily. At one end of the pool was a tower with three levels of diving boards.

Mike Russell and I decided to climb to the topmost level, but when we got there we had second thoughts about diving from such a height.

We were about to descend to a lower level when a vision of loveliness appeared at the edge of the pool.

Mike and I were not about to slink to a lower level, not with that lovely lady looking on. We assumed it was the Jones' daughter, clad in a skin-tight form-fitting bathing suit. At her appearance, silence descended, eyes bulged and all activity ceased.

After showing us what we were fighting for, she dove in, swam to the opposite side of the pool, swam back, got out of the pool, picked up her towel and strolled leisurely to the house. Action exploded once again and the fun went on.

Then it was time to leave Jamshedpur, and we bid goodbye to Mrs. Jones, with all of us glowing with pleasant memories of the afternoon. But, what of Mike and me and the high diving board? No way were we about to show cowardice in full view of that lovely gal— we jumped from that scary height and hit

the water like two cinder blocks, narrowly missing a couple of swimmers who were unaware of our ungainly descent.

This was more dangerous than bombing the Gokteik Viaduct. (Who said war is hell?)

NEPALESE VACATION
SHANGRI LA?

Some time in the summer of 1943, Elmer Thompson, Wendell Hanson and I got a few days off from our duties in Chakulia, India, and decided to vacation for a short time in the cool mountains of Darjeeling.

We boarded a train in Chakulia and arrived in Calcutta where we entrained for the long trip to the foot of the Himalayan Mountains. Upon arrival at that station, we hired a taxi to take us to another station, where we were to board another train to take us up the mountain to Darjeeling. On the taxi trip we were treated to the thrill of encountering a herd of wild elephants that materialized from the nearby jungle and briefly stopped our forward progress.

As we drove along, a monkey materialized and stood in the middle of the road, chattering and gnashing his teeth. Our driver stopped and we watched to see what the monkey would do. It was clear that he was threatening us. He then looked to his right and barked. This resulted in a female monkey carrying her young who emerged timorously and joined the male. He barked again and his mate and her baby scooted into the jungle.

It was then that we noticed the beautiful orchids entwined around the trees lining the jungle road. The sight was not lost upon Elmer Thompson, Wendell Hanson and me. The myriad colors were enchanting.

On the narrow-gauge rail train we chugged up the steep grade, negotiating scary hairpin turns, at times backing up, changing rails, on to sharp "ess" turns, backing up again and again in order to make the tortuous ascent.

We finally arrived at the top of our particular mountain resort.

We found a place to stay at a private home, where we were made welcome by Mrs. Mackey, the owner of a fine, spacious home. Elmer, Wendell and I spent our first night in an enormous bedroom. There was no central heating but a huge fireplace made the room livable. We were warm as toast during the night but when morning dawned, the fire had gone out and the room became dank and cold. The three of us stared at

each other, under covers, waiting to see which one of us had the guts to get up and shower in what would assuredly be icy water.

But then—reprieve with the arrival of a Nepalese bearer carrying a huge tray with a pot of piping hot coffee as well as jams, jellies, toast and oranges.

This repast was meant only to strengthen our resolve to get out of bed and to shower and shave and THEN go to a real breakfast of freshly caught trout, fried tomatoes, more coffee, toast, jams and marmalades.

Our Nepalese bearer, whom we promptly named Friday, was trying to start a fire in the fireplace, but the hard wood stubbornly refused to ignite. He used up all his matches and left to get some

more. I don't recall which one of us sprinkled lighter fluid on the wood but when the bearer returned Wendell waved Friday away and with great aplomb, lit a match and touched it to the fluid-soaked wood; it instantly burst into flame. The poor bearer jumped ten feet in the air and looked upon us with fear and awe. For the rest of our stay at Mrs. Mackey's, he was quite circumspect in his dealings with us.

Like many other tourists, we prowled around after stowing our gear in Mrs. Mackey's mountaintop home where we spent our vacation period. One early morning we heard the skirling of bagpipes. Mrs. Mackey informed us that a Scottish group of soldiers played bagpipes and put on a precision drill each morning on the village square. We three hurried over and caught at least the final half of the performance. Dressed in plaid caps and skirts, knee-high socks and snow-white shoes, the group of Scots enthralled the civilian and military vacationers with their intricate drill maneuvers. There is something captivating and wild about the skirling of bagpipes. There was a British military cantonment about a thousand feet lower on the mountain and we assumed that was where this group of Scots came from.

After the Scots left the area, a group of Indians rode in on horseback. It was a sheik and his contingent of ten or twelve compatriots all astride milk white horses. They had come to the Gymkhana Club for their daily tennis matches.

On another day we ventured down the mountainside and found a pub. It was full of Tommies and it didn't take long for us to realize that we weren't welcome there. Back we went up the mountainside. We saw native workers picking leaves off stubby bushes. This was where the famous Darjeeling Tea had its origin.

The next morning arrived along with the clanging of bells swung by lamas dressed in orange colored gowns. Strings of prayer beads encircled their waists. Mrs. Mackey had prepared us for this daily event; what were expected of us were alms. We donated a few rupees into a brass cup held out by the lamas. They bowed and muttered a few words, which I took to be a blessing. Mrs. Mackey had warned us to give alms to lamas, as strange things happen to people who fail to give something, no matter how little, to these religious mendicants.

On our walks we visited a Buddhist temple where a lama, in hushed tones, explained the meaning of various sacred objects and also answered our questions.

On a nearby knoll was a prayer tree where there was a constant stiff breeze. Pieces of cloth and paper were attached to the limbs and all fluttered wildly. This was good, we were told. The gusts of wind swiftly carried written supplications to Buddha for as long as the wind blew. I personally marveled at how greatly religion colored the Nepalese' daily life.

We were present for an annual religious experience but the best I could do was to get no closer to the bloodletting event than the outermost fringe of the crowd. I did manage to spot the dancer who gyrated in the middle of the crowd. It was a man wearing a wig and a dress, mascara, lipstick with cheeks brightly rouged. In the center of the mob was a bull, a noose around its neck. As several men pulled on its tail, others pulled the noose to stretch the unfortunate animal's neck. A man with a scimitar was to cut the bull's head off with one blow. I couldn't stomach this so I didn't watch. A roar from the crowd attested to the fact that the head was severed with only one blow. The picture I had of this event is long gone and only a memory remains. I often wonder if the Nepalese lifestyle is still the same or if that nation succumbed to the inexorable vagaries of the march of time and change as could be expected.

At the Gymkhana Club on our mountain top, we were made welcome to use the club's facilities, including the game room, bar and billiard tables. We were even invited to attend the Saturday night dance. There, joviality reigned supreme and imbibing copious quantities of the cup that cheers insured that. The revelers were British officers and various ethnic groups of civilians. As the evening wore on, frequent visitors to the bar helped to keep the party loud and lively. We three were dragged on to the dance floor, where we did the boomps-a-daisy with the best of them. Sometime between our second and third drinks (or was it six or seven?), Wendell noticed the chandelier swaying and attributed it to the drinks we were enjoying. Without further ado, he marched to the open fireplace and threw his glass into it—Elmer and I decided to do the same and the resulting tinkling of shattered glass brought the merrymaking on the dance floor to an abrupt halt, and the thunderous silence and chilly stares shriveled us to abject mortification. Wendell whispered to me, "Isn't that what they do in the movies—break the glasses in the fireplace?"

"Only when proposing a toast," I whispered back.

After a short while, the dancing resumed and we gladly left the area and went into the game room where a jolly Englishman asked us what we thought of the earthquake we just experienced—an event that happens quite frequently in the

Himalayas he assured us. Elmer, Wendell and I looked at each other dumbfounded; it wasn't the drinks after all—the floor and ceiling did indeed heave and roll, but it was the earthquake and not our drinks that was responsible; we promptly marched back to the bar to correct some business that was unfinished.

My children asked, "What did you do in the war, Daddy?" It had been hard to explain that you dropped bombs that assuredly cut short some people's lives. I try not to color war experiences as glamorous or heroic. I like to think that they prefer my tales, such as this one, that recall experiences that are, for the most part, less inclined toward violence and mayhem.

DARJEELING RACES

At one of our daily exploratory forays during our vacation trip to Darjeeling, we wandered to a racetrack, which we were told was the highest racetrack in the world. The horses were tiny racing ponies and the jockeys were tiny and couldn't have weighed more than 75 pounds soaking wet.

Bets were being made with much shouting and gesticulating, along with additions, subtractions and multiplications on slate tote boards. The numbers written with chalk were erased and re-written again and again. The shouting of the men accepting the bets and the yelling of the bettors left us mystified.

We wandered over to the paddock to look over the ponies and to decide which ones to bet on. After making our selections we went back to make our bets. The action continued fast and furious, and the hullabaloo of people trying to get their bets down in time was puzzling to us. We made bets not knowing which ponies we were backing.

Unbeknown to us, two young Indian ladies were watching us in amusement and giggling at our seeming lack of expertise in placing our bets. They could see we were not knowledgeable gamblers—in India, anyway. Finally, one of them came up to me and, in perfect English, asked me how much I wished to bet.

I gave her a fist full of rupees and told her the number of the pony I wanted to bet on. She assured me it was a bad selection, plus the odds were not good. She bet my money on her selection

and to the best of my recollection that pony is still running, while my original selection romped home a winner. Well, as the races went on, we bet on ponies they selected for us and the girls lost their money as well as ours.

The girls appeared to be well educated and were quite prim and proper, so we were a bit surprised when they invited us to their home in Calcutta, to meet their parents. What a home—it took over most of a city block. Earlier, the girls had informed me that their daddy owned a large number of Calcutta's apartment buildings, which he rented out to various departments of the Allied armed forces. I was interested to see how the upper class lived in India.

When we arrived at the house, the parents and guests were playing bridge in a huge play room. After acknowledging us in a perfunctory manner, they went back to their bridge game. A young man entered the room and nodded stiffly to us upon being introduced by his sisters. In order to make conversation, I inquired if he was a student or a member of the British armed forces. "My dear boy," he sniffed, "I am an Indian and have no interest in the war at all. I am leaving tonight to travel to England to pursue my studies at Oxford."

After being thoroughly squelched, we made our excuses and left for the Chowringee railroad station for our trip back to Chakulia.

A VISIT TO YANGKAI VILLAGE

As they must, at one time or another, second lieutenants get assigned to officer of the day duty, which meant checking the perimeter and revetment areas of the base. In addition, the duties include checking the mess halls for the "quality" of the food and counting the prisoners in the stockade, if there are any at the beginning and end of the tour of duty.

Accompanied by an MP (military police) sergeant, a Jeep driver, plus a corporal riding "shot gun," we drove to the "metropolis" of Yangkai. Checking the village was only a token gesture because I doubted if there were any Romeos at our base who would be scouting around for romance. If there were any wanderers who visited the village

Our slow trip through the village didn't turn up any problems; the village had just the one main street, a dirt road and no sidewalks. Running around energetically were youngsters whose

ages I judged to run the gamut of five years to eleven. Almost all were lighting and shooting firecrackers. Evidently, not for any special occasion—it appeared that sort of activity is a daily occurrence. All the children were armed with firecrackers of uniform size and just shot them off for the hell of it. The youngest of them wore a pajama-like outfit with a convenient slit in the back for the express purpose of taking care of mother nature's demands if, as and when the spirit came upon them. But, "waste not, want not"—each made certain he or she duly contributed to a nearby night soil depository.

Incidentally, that turned me off Chinese vegetables, when I found that human waste product was used as a garden fertilizer.

As it was rapidly growing dark, oil lamps began to appear in windows and as the yellowish lights came on, the story "Oil for the Lamps of China" ran through my mind. The windows had no curtains and we could see activities within. In one particular building, somewhat larger than the others in the area, I spied wizened old men with wispy beards sipping their tea as they sat at long tables—in a large room; the flickering light of the oil lamps gave the room a mysterious glow.

The men carried on animated conversations, in between long, thoughtful puffs on their curved clay pipes. I couldn't help

but wonder what earth-shaking events were under discussion. But they were so far away from the war zone, their bucolic existence seemed so serene, so stable and so predictable that one could only imagine that they were immersed in local gossip with occasional references to the thoughts and writings of Confucius.

And—what were they thinking of us, we strangers from a far off land? Did they even bother to give us a passing thought? Were they glad to have us in their midst, or did our presence annoy them? Our noisy warplanes taking off and landing nearby—what did they think of them? They were, after all, simple villagers isolated from other small towns by many miles with no telephones, no electricity, no public transportation; a sort of Shangri La nestled in the foothills of the surrounding hills.

As we drove away and on to the airstrip, a chill wind blew across open spaces, biting and penetrating—my leather flight jacket did not offer much protection. We stopped some distance away from each revetment and I left the Jeep to walk in the darkness to each plane and checked out the area by the light of my flashlight. At one particular revetment I knew I was in big trouble when I realized that the six or seven Chinese in long coats and felt boots with turned up toes who suddenly surrounded me were Chinese bandits, a breed of bandits not noted for their gentle and compassionate hearts.

Their sudden appearance from the darkness startled me and their scowling faces bode me no good. Rifles grasped firmly in their hands held close to their chests, fingers on triggers was very disconcerting.

The MP's sprawled in the vehicle fifty feet away were completely unaware of my predicament. I tried to appear relaxed and at ease as I smiled at the strangers glaring at me and offered them chewing gum and cigarettes which they mutely accepted, their faces impassive under their cone-shaped hats. Not knowing what their intentions were I let out a yell, "Hey sergeant, get up here on the double and bring your weapons—I'm surrounded."

The reassuring shout from the MP, "Coming right up, lieutenant," was the most welcome sound I could ever hope to hear and it had an immediate effect on the motley crew surrounding me; they disappeared into the darkness as quickly and as silently as they materialized a few moments before.

The incident was duly reported upon return to the base and within minutes, a ten-wheeler loaded with whooping and yelling GIs went roaring to the air strip and on up the road into the hills, all of them armed with a variety of weapons, BAR's, shot guns, rifles, carbines and Colt 45's.

This was an exciting adventure they all wanted to be a part of, a welcome respite from monotony that is sometimes part of military life. I waved to them as they roared out to do battle with the bad guys. I, of course, did not volunteer to join the posse, as I had enough excitement for the day.

Needless to say, their quarry was long gone by the time they arrived at the scene of my uncomfortable confrontation in those dark foothills of western China. In retelling this story in the safety of my home, I ask myself in amazement, "Was that really me, so far from home, and did I really experience that hair-raising incident? Did it really happen?"

Recurring dreams attest to that.

TRIBUTE TO ZED BARNES

It was a cool, crisp day in February; there was a slight breeze and the sun was still low on the horizon. Mike Russell and I were trudging up the mountainside toting our firearms; he with an M-16 and I with a .25 caliber carbine. We both carried our Colt 45's in shoulder holsters, so we felt adequately armed to face whatever game we encountered in the western mountains of China. We had decided the day before that we would go hunting and now we were on our way a few miles from the village of Yangkai, China.

On the way up the mountain we were accosted by a Chinese lad who appeared to be about twelve or thirteen years of age. He noted our firearms and by much pointing and various gestures, he informed us that he was willing to be our guide and would help us find game. We had no idea what game he was gesturing about but nevertheless we agreed to have him accompany us as our guide. Some distance up the mountain we noticed caves in the sides of the mountain, some overgrown by brush and some hidden in depressions and barely visible in the terrain.

At one point the lad started yelling and throwing stones into one cave that was in full view; after having thrown several stones he ran in back of us as if looking for safety. Totally mystified, Mike and I laid down our arms and walked up to the cave and peered in. It was totally dark and we could see nothing of the interior, so we too started to throw stones into it. With that, the lad let out a screech and went flying down the mountain, slipping and falling all the way.

141

We found out later that these caves were the haunts of wild boars and that if one was in there it could have ripped Mike and me into shreds before we could get to our guns, which were several feet away from us. Luckily for both of us, the cave happened to be empty and we two bonehead nimrods were spared what could have been a tragedy.

After roaming around the mountainside for a couple of hours, we became bored and started to shoot at trees and rocks. Mike had criss-crossed his soft nose bullets effectively, making them into dum-dums. Firing at trees and saplings, they did enormous damage and made us marvel at the awful damage they would make in hitting a human on any part of his body. Eventually, we decided to come off the mountain.

As we drew near the village we spied several old Chinese women at the side of the road. They sat and seemed to be taking a rest break. I noticed their feet, which were bound with cloth and looked no bigger than a normal fist. They prepared to leave to continue their journey and each one of them needed help rising. Then, they tottered along and appeared in imminent danger of falling if they stopped their forward motion.

Upon reaching the base and having turned in our weapons to the provost marshal, we went into the mess hall to catch a cup of coffee and possibly a piece of toast, as the dinner hour was long past. In the hall was Zed Barnes, the squadron adjutant, and an air force doctor and they were deep in conversation over cups of coffee. The doctor was apparently a transient on his way down the line to his permanent post. As we all sat in the gloom, a staff sergeant came puffing in; he seemed to be under emotional stress. He approached Zed and blurted out that he had shot an old

Chinese woman. Zed calmed him down and finally the story came out.

It seems the sergeant and some buddies also had gone up the mountain and on the way back were shooting their Colt 45's at rocks and trees. One of his bullets ricocheted and struck an old woman in the stomach and she was found lying on the side of the road. Zed asked the doctor to go look at the woman and got a prompt refusal from the doctor. But Zed was persistent and the

doctor went to see what he could do for the poor old lady who I thought didn't have a chance, knowing what a 45 slug can do to a human body.

I never found out the details of this drama, but did hear that the doctor operated on the woman and she miraculously recovered.

Somewhere, there is a former staff sergeant enjoying peace of mind for not causing the death of an innocent human being and I wonder if in his prayers at night, he thanks God for putting a Zed Barnes on this earth.

SEA SWEEP

The preparation for a high level bombing mission, its execution and return to base are an exciting experience. But after a combat man's missions number 50 or 60, it can boil down to a dull routine. Nevertheless, each step is given just as much care and caution as ever. And there is always that tightening up when the target is sighted and the bombing run has begun. This is where training comes to the fore; ack-ack, fighters, nothing distracts the crew from the few vital moments when the bombardier is lining up the target and the pilot is flying the PDI (Pilot Direction Indicator). After "Bombs Away," everyone settles down to watchful waiting until the home base comes under the wings. In essence, it is, "Take off, hit your target, and come home."

That was my attitude when I went on my first low altitude mission out of Yangkai as bombardier-navigator. To say I got plenty of excitement is putting it mildly—and I do mean mildly. I'll try to put down on paper all the events during a low level bombing mission off the China coast. We were on the prowl for Jap shipping.

We had taken off early in the morning, in a four ship formation. I was in B-2 position, with 1st Lt. Howard Feigley at the controls. "B" Flight leader was 1st Lt. David K. Hayward, a cool, level-headed boy from Pasadena, Calif. Ten minutes out, we ran into bad weather and climbed up to 13,000 feet to get on top of the overcast. Never once did we see the ground.

When we reached our ETA (estimated time of arrival), we flew two minutes beyond our DR (dead reckoning) position, and began our let down. We broke through at 2,000 feet over the water and continued down.

We got down so low that we could smell the salt sea air. As we skimmed over the waves, the Chinese fishermen in their sampans looked up and waved—their faces creased in wide smiles.

After a systematic, but fruitless search for Jap boats, we headed for the coast and spied a 200 foot Jap freighter, tied up at a dock in Vinh harbor. 1st Lt. Elmer C. Thompson, "A" Flight Leader, led the whole formation over the ship and we strafed it from stem to stern. He then turned off, followed by Lt. Hayward, leaving two planes to take care of that "sitting duck." A-2, flown by Mike Russell and B-2 (Lt. Feigley) then made a tight turn to the right to come in at the ship on its port side.

A-2 (Mike) came in at mast-high level, with all of its guns blazing away, and rammed a 500 pounder into its side. Brown smoke boiled out of the center of the ship, and it listed badly. B-2 (Feigley), following closely behind, repeated the performance.

During the melee, a lone Jap machine gun chattered from the afterdeck. What damage it did we didn't find out until we landed at our home base.

A-2 (Mike) peeled off after its run and took off for home. But we, in B-2, weren't satisfied and came around for another crack at the ship. As we came at the ship, I could see that it had broken in two, and the front end was under water. The mast stuck up at a crazy angle; as we roared in, I looked up and saw the mast directly in front of me. I don't think a giant tree in the Redwood Forest of California looked any bigger to an ant than that misplaced telephone pole looked to me. I got on interphone and screamed to the pilot, "For gosh sake, pull up." In the split second before we hit, I pictured in my mind's eye a very unsavory scene; that of Lt. Feigley climbing out of the cockpit and nonchalantly telling the crew chief, "Scrape out the bombardier's greenhouse and fill up the gas tanks, please."

But the pilot's reactions were as fast as our speed of closure; he pulled up and, as a result, we just scraped our bottom on the top of the mast. About six inches of the mast were left in the radio compartment, however, making a jagged hole on the underside of our fuselage. Just as we hit, Sgt. Arthur O. Routhier, the turret gunner, and S/Sgt. Lloyd J. Sleeth, the radio gunner, got on the interphone, yelling unintelligibly. The pilot was too busy flying the ship, so I called them back and asked them to call in to me, one at a time. The radio man called and this is what I could make out of his words, which were shouted in one continuous sentence. "Sir, the tail gunner is wounded; he's not hurt bad, I don't think; wait, he's acting silly; jeez, we just hit the mast; there's a big hole in the rear; I'll go see how he is; boy, oh boy!!" plus a few unprintable.

With a little patient questioning, I found that a bullet had hit the Plexiglas beside Sgt. Charles A. Davison, the tail gunner, cleared his head by about an inch, and then passed through the fuselage directly above him. The shattered Plexiglas sprayed his face and hands and caused numerous minor cuts. However, it was more uncomfortable than serious, as Davison spent the next two days in and out of the squadron dispensary, having bits of glass excavated from his skin. As the bullet left the ship, it ripped through the aluminum, and he was so close that the wind whipped his hair into the hole. This was what had the boys in the rear really excited. So, what with the tail gunner's close shave and coming home with an actual piece of mast from the Jap boat, the gunners aft of the bomb bay cried "Aye," when S/Sgt. Joe Sleeth of Arkansas City, Kansas, said, "The black soil of Kansas never looked sweeter than the red dust of China does this afternoon!!!"

Getting back to the mission, we then found a railroad and followed it until we spotted a bridge. We still had three bombs left so we made a run on the bridge. On our first run the bombs wouldn't release, so Feigley racked the plane around and we made another run. Meanwhile, a Jap machine gun was firing at us from the west end of the bridge; the tracers cutting across our path could be seen plainly. I dumped our bombs in salvo on the bridge and lost no time getting out of there. I gave the pilot a heading to fly and we were off for home.

On our return we were met by sober-faced men instead of the usual cheerful grins. The copilot in A-2 had been hit by the machine gun on the deck of that Jap freighter and he died on the way to the home base. It was a sad blow to an otherwise successful mission. Lt. Hugh R. Harrison, bombardier-navigator of A-2, administered first aid promptly, but it was of no avail. The copilot, Robert K. Barron, died in his arms, up in the blue that the copilot loved so well.

That was my first low altitude mission—scare, death and sadness. How do we feel about it? Sgt. Tony Mercep summed it up aptly for all of us when he said, "Just keep giving me a crack at those ... that's all I ask!!!"

A ONE-ARM TONY MERCEP

Tony Mercep was on the same mission, although in a different plane, when Howard Feigley flew our plane into the mast of a ship which we skip-bombed. Dave Hayward would recollect that incident, as we were flying on his wing.

Well, I was scheduled to be returned stateside before Tony. He had previously sent home a snapshot of himself leaning against a Jeep, with one arm hidden behind his back. His mother was frantic as she believed Tony had an arm blown off. His letter to her did not convince her that he was not hurt and he implored me to travel to his home on Long Island and tell her personally that he was alive and well and unhurt. I did just that and received the royal treatment from the Mercep family.

Elmer C. "Tommy" Thompson
LOOKING AT THE
TOP OF THE WORLD

There are many things for those of us in the 22nd Bomb Squadron to remember. One experience comes to mind that involved Steve Stankiewicz, Wendell Hanson and me. We were given a few days off duty for a rest leave after we had been in Chakulia for some months.

We started our trip on the train in Calcutta, bound for the far northeastern corner of India. From there, we boarded a narrow gauge train that took us from a couple hundred feet above sea level to almost eight thousand feet, when we arrived at Darjeeling. This train trip took us through a number of climate changes as we quickly gained altitude. We traveled from the hot, dry plains of India through a jungle-type area where we saw monkeys, large elephants and other wild animals.

The train was able to move up to higher elevations by using a series of switch backs. The switch backs would allow the train to move up as far as it could go in one direction and then back the train in the opposite direction gaining some altitude with each series. One of the things I remember was the young native boys running along the back of the train and staying with us until they were given some baksheesh (gifts of money).

At Darjeeling we found ourselves at 8,000 feet above sea level and observing one of the finest views of anything in this entire world. Mt. Kanchenjunga, about 40 miles away, stood among a whole range of mountains, each above 25,000 feet. Mt. Kanchenjunga, at 28,169 feet, was the highest peak visible.

Darjeeling is a place where wealthy Anglo-Indian families from such places as Calcutta would go for long holidays to get relief from the terribly hot weather on the plains. There were lots of things going on in the way of entertainment, such as horse racing, gambling and other things that well-heeled people like to do.

This was quite a change from life at our base in India. We met some young adults who attended schools in Europe and the U.S. and now their world-wide travels were limited due to the war. They were stuck in India for the duration.

Needing a place to stay, we were fortunate in being able to contact the widow of a British military officer who operated a guest house. She allowed us to stay there for our leave. One of the problems which we ran into immediately was that a servant was not traveling with us. She informed us, in no uncertain terms, that it was absolutely necessary for us to have a servant to make our beds, serve us meals in the dining room, and keep things tidy.

This was quickly solved by the lady of the house who just happened to know of a young native boy from Nepal who could look after us. We became closely attached to the young boy. When we left, he wanted to go with us. We could have adopted him on the spot and hated to leave him.

The one thing that stood out on this trip above all else was the seeing of Mt. Everest. We could not see this mountain from Darjeeling, even though it was close by. It was necessary for us to go to Tiger Mountain to be able to see Mt. Everest. Tiger Mountain has an elevation of about 8,500 feet. This meant leaving Darjeeling a couple of hours before daybreak and going by taxi to the top of Tiger Mountain.

At that time, everything was dark. As daylight approached, the light from the sun hit the peaks of the world's tallest mountains, one by one, the first being Mt. Everest, the highest of course, while everything else was dark below. As the sun continued to rise, the peaks of this tallest mountain range would burst into bright light glowing as gold while the rest of the area was still in total darkness. The first thing we could see was the very tip of Mt. Everest, all golden, next, Mt. Kanchenjunga all aglow, and then all the other peaks in that range, one by one, appeared in gold. What a magnificent sight to see!

This trip has many stories which are worth telling, but this one is surely the highlight. It is a shame that places such as this are in so remote an area, so difficult to get to, a sight so magnificent as this one, hidden in that remote part of the world! I feel very blessed to have been able to see it in late 1943.

Wendell H. Hanson
OVERSEAS EXPRESS

One year after I began pilot training, our crew was on its way to West Palm Beach, Florida, for overseas shipment. It had all been serious fun and games, but now the excitement became electric. We knew that we would ship out by air, but what aircraft? Where? When? We found out the "when." In three days. We prepared for the royal "fly away" with a series of parties, hundreds of officers and men, all in various stages of partying.

I noticed our crew was riding bicycles. I asked Fred Stowers, "Where did we get these wheels?" Grinning, he said, "Don't you remember, we bought them this morning." That sounded reasonable.

The next day I awakened and looked for my wrist watch, but I could not see it. I slid my right hand up and down the left forearm. Still no watch. Stowers was standing in my doorway, still grinning. He held out my watch and slid it over my hand. I never asked what happened. Perhaps I just do not wish to know.

It was the day we were leaving the United States, the ZI (the Zone of Interior). But first, a complete physical exam had to take place for one hundred and fifty stripped-naked crewmen, none of which were in very good shape at the time. We admitted there was an eye chart on the wall, but it seemed that nobody could read it. It's fortunate that we were to ride into South America rather than drive.

Twenty-five crewmen and Captain Taffy (my Cocker Spaniel puppy) boarded a four-engine C-54 commercial passenger plane and flew to Borenquin Field, Puerto Rico. That evening we checked the bar drinks. Large Cokes were a nickel and double Scotch on the rocks priced out at ten cents. I limited my crew to one drink because we were going to see the world and countries that we may otherwise only read about in books. I didn't win any popularity poll, but the crew officers said it turned out to be a good idea.

Perhaps sixty-five C-54s were used to shuttle military passengers both ways on the express. We had different planes and crews on certain segments of our trip. It was everyday back-and-forth fast transportation from July, 1942, until September, 1945. It was the first sustained operation of a world airline.

In the middle of the Atlantic Ocean lay Ascension Island (UK), the tip of a centuries-old volcano with barely enough room for six aircraft and a single short runway for takeoff and landing. We could never fly across the South Atlantic without this small airport. At the end of the runway, there was a 200-foot drop into the South Atlantic and the sharks were waiting. There was no chance of rescue or survival if you did not have proper air speed on takeoff. On that cinder-top volcano you just had time to use the latrine and it was, "Gas up and go." Soldiers stationed there should get a special medal.

Officers at Aden, in present-day Yemen, stressed the danger along the 1,000 mile south coast of Arabia. There was absolutely no way to help any crew that had to ditch their plane. The natives were restless, like sharks, we were told. However, we arrived safely at Karachi, India, and made the trip back on the same route a year later.

CROSSING INDIA

Karachi, a city in what is now Pakistan on the coast of the Arabian Sea, is located a few miles north of the Tropic of Cancer. It gave us a first look at the crush of humanity that is India. Seven hundred miles east and slightly north lay Agra, probably the cleanest city in India.

The city of Agra is just south of New Delhi, which was the headquarters for the 10th Air Force and gateway to the China-Burma-India war zone. We stopped in Agra for three days while our final assignment was decided upon. We toured this strange city and eventually located the famed Taj Mahal. Magnificent! The Taj Mahal is a masterpiece of marble buildings with an entrance pool about 60 feet wide and 300 feet long, bordered by walkways of marble.

A prince, or Maharaja, built this beautiful mausoleum as a stately tomb for his Maharani. The one large room inside has two marble caskets for viewing. However, they are empty now, and the royal couple is buried in caskets twenty feet below. We climbed steps inside two of the minarets where the Muslims were called to worship each morning and evening. The Taj Mahal alone is worth a trip to India.

Captain Taffy, that cute Cocker Spaniel, flew with us almost half way around the world. At every stop, one of us carried him off the plane to the bus or truck, and then tied him to a bed post in a secure hostel guarded by U. S. Army personnel. Engine noise disturbed him, so he curled up on his sleeping pad whenever we flew. In Agra, he was tethered to my bed post and the door was locked whenever I was out of the barracks. Captain Taffy was

157

stolen on our first day in Agra. I offered a 300 rupee ($100) reward, equal to more than one year of income for a Hindu family. It seemed that half of the people in that city searched for him. Some Maharaja probably bought him. I wasn't very happy. Who would stoop to steal our mascot??

We were next flown 700 miles south-south-east to Dum Dum Airfield at Calcutta, and had just enough time to transfer equipment and personal belongings to a DC3 for our final flight to Chakulia, 100 miles to the west. The trouble was, I had a case of fast trots at Dum Dum and ran to the latrine. Just made it. Then more trouble. I heard our transport start its engines. I shagged out, holding my pants with one hand, cap in the other, saw a lieutenant lounging against the building, saw the plane start to

taxi, ran past the lieutenant and said, "Hi," noticed he was a bird colonel, snapped him a half-ass salute with cap in my right hand, and waved my cap at the DC3 which stopped and picked me up. No doubt that colonel is still laughing. He couldn't have been over 25 years old. It's the war, stupid!

CHAKULIA, INDIA

We arrived March 28, 1943, and were assigned to the 22nd Bomb Squadron, one of four squadrons in the 341st Bomb Group. Original ground support had departed for India on two troop ships. The SS Mariposa left Charleston, South Carolina, on May 28, 1942, and arrived at Karachi on July 25, 1942. HMS Mauritania departed Newport News, Virginia, on Oct. 7, 1942, and arrived at Ceylon. Army personnel then changed to the City of Paris, a 10,500 ton coal-fired India coastal steamer, and arrived at Karachi on December 2, 1942. By truck and train they traveled over 1,200 miles to Chakulia. B-25s and their crews began arriving in September, 1942, forming the 11th, 22nd, 490th and 491st Bomb Squadrons. The Burma campaign began.

Before we venture into combat, let's examine Chakulia, a virtual boondocks right in the middle of agricultural and forest land. The nearby town of Jamshedpur was twenty miles northwest. We were at latitude 23 degrees, the same as Mazatlan, Mexico, very near the Tropic of Cancer. It was hot, hot, hot for this northern-plains, Norwegian, Dane, Scot, Irish, English, and Dutch-bred American. The monsoons doused us with 102 inches of rain. That's 8 ½ feet of water. Someone "borrowed" my raincoat when the rain began and two months later I found it on a peg in the officers' club. The rain, of course, had stopped.

The first lunch in the mess hall was surprisingly good, especially the caraway seed bread. Marvelous. On the second day, I noticed some of those seeds moved. I stopped and studied that bread. I glanced at the lieutenant seated next to me who had been with the squadron a few months. He looked at me, grinned and said, "I wondered how long it would take before you caught on. Go on, eat it. Great protein." It was a week before I gave in. That batch of bread lasted another ten days.

India was part of the British Empire and they had charge of doling out all food rations, including American shipments. The Brits took all our strawberry and blackberry  jam and sent us the orange marmalade. They didn't earn any brownie points from me.

I have a problem concerning snakes and India has more than its share. Poisonous Kraits are little finger snakes that like to curl up for a nap in warm, dark places, like the toe of a shoe. Every morning we poked a stick into the toe area, then stomped the heel on the concrete floor, just hoping. Cobras seem to be everywhere. One morning I wrapped a towel around me, slipped on clog shoes and walked toward the latrine. Thank God, Red Moore from Findley, Ohio, was walking beside me. Suddenly he shoved me hard into the cinders. Bruised and bleeding, I got up and stared at my next step—a small fourteen-inch cobra and I would have stepped on it. If you are bitten, try counting to ten.

One night I was awakened by deep, rapid breathing. I glanced toward the wall and dresser opposite my bed. Some big-eyed, three foot tall animal was staring right back. I grabbed my loaded revolver from under the pillow and pulled off five fast shots. Four had gone through three walls and three rooms of the basha. My friends were in an uproar. The fifth shot hit the dresser. I had missed. The next morning our native bearers checked the paw prints and said, "Hyena." On a ranking of one to ten as a place to live, India ranks a minus fifteen.

Considering the war situation, we had excellent quarters. The bashas (huts) were constructed with a bamboo frame and thatched roof. Walls between the seven rooms, each fourteen by seventeen feet in size, were split bamboo covered with a mixture of mud and sand with a little cement. Each room had front and rear screen doors and windows. Each basha rested on a concrete slab. The pleasant surprises were the electric lights in each room. It was a couple of weeks before I was told why I had received an end room with single bed, small table with lamp, dresser and desk—but no roommate. I questioned a friend and with some prodding he said, "Well, Hanson, everyone is a little superstitious. They know you lost roommates at every training field." Enough said.

Aper (A pair) and Konkea were our house boys who lived in the other end room of our basha. We paid each of them to make the beds, clean the rooms and handle the laundry. One evening they came charging out of their room, shouting like lunatics to everyone, "Tiger, tiger, our room." Pistols out, officers poured out of every room and very carefully approached their quarters. No tiger. It had jumped through a screen window to get in, but it probably escaped through the door. We considered alerting the squadron to commandeer Jeeps and surround a large area, then close the circle. Somebody said, "Bad idea. If we saw the tiger, we would all start shooting and kill half the squadron." That ended the proposed hunt.

Single beds were constructed with two by fours and a rope mesh, which held a four inch thick straw tick mattress. Six foot long split bamboo poles were fastened to each corner. A screen canopy was stretched over the top of the poles and down to the sides of the straw tick, and then tucked under. This did a great job of keeping mosquitoes away. We slept with a flashlight and pistol under the pillow.

In the tropics I wore boxer shorts to bed and rarely used a sheet. One night I had settled down, tucked in the netting and dozed. But wait a minute; something heavy is clinging to the rope net under the straw tick. I could feel it moving around, grasping different ropes. That made me sweat. Bombardier-navigators Fred Stowers and Bob Yeck were in the next room and I called, "Hey Fred, will you check out what is crawling around just under my bed?" He came in, flashed his light, muttered something and went back to his room. *Well,* I thought, *it must be some kind of harmless animal, but I can't be sure.* I picked up the pistol, pulled away the netting, jumped out of bed, raced across the room, turned on the light and glanced under the bed. No. It could not be a rat. But it was a very big rat. I chased it around the room and clubbed it.

Nobody told us, we just assumed that Chakulia Air Base might be a target for Jap bombers. A five foot deep slit trench was twenty feet from our basha, ready for any careless soldier walking around after dark. We discussed the possible use of the trench and the subject of snakes was duly considered. All had spent an hour or two studying the three foot by three foot colored chart showing fifteen snakes and a graphic description of each. Some were very poisonous; others just poisonous and a few were non-poisonous. It was agreed by all in our basha that we would treat all snakes as poisonous.

We also decided to take our chances with Jap bombers rather than to jump in that slit trench, which surely must be a haven for vipers. No one ever fell or jumped in. No Jap bombers ever came to Chakulia.

The officers club was a basha about 20 feet by 100 feet with several tables and chairs and a bar that served warm gin and lime drinks in metal glasses. That combination tasted like a warm metallic lime with a kick. Absolutely, incontrovertibly the most dissatisfying excuse for a bar drink that was ever invented or dispensed. I had two sips, the second just to prove how bad it tasted. No more. We invited English officers from the local ack-ack battery to the club. They thought we had good taste in offering gin and lime drinks. Warm. We wanted to get rid of the stuff and hope something better would show up in the next truck of provisions. No luck, but the Brits were happy.

Bad weather and one mission a week filled the club with bridge players in the afternoon and poker or dice from 1830 to 2300. I watched a few Red Dog games and fortunately decided never to play.

Major Robert S. Puckett had played Red Dog, losing heavily. He was the squadron commander and returned to the zone of the interior (U.S.A.) a couple of months after I arrived. He sent back checks every month we were in Chakulia, paying Red Dog debts. I played straight poker and six card high-low and built up a healthy stake.

COMBAT MISSIONS
FROM INDIA

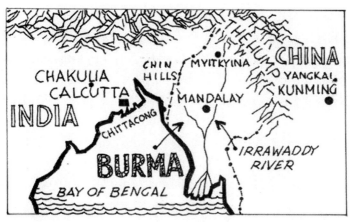

While in India, all combat missions were confined to Burma. From Chakulia it is 300 miles to the Chin Hills, then 100 miles over the Chin Hills to Burma. The Chin Hills are an extension of the Himalaya Mountains from their north point at 17,000 feet, gradually decreasing south to 4,000 feet where they meet the Bay of Bengal, completely separating India from Burma.

The British lost Burma to the Jap invaders in 1942, but they left a great spy system in place. British and American ground forces were filtering back to Burma and they needed air strikes at Myitkyina (Mishenaw), a major Burmese city. Spies recommended that the 10th Air Force should bomb Japanese troops in a vast housing complex near the Mali River front at 1930 hours. Six B25C aircraft covered the area with 500 pound bombs and brought back pictures of the destruction. Our intelligence officer, Major Arther, said we had destroyed at least 2,000 Japanese troops—in the red light district. Probably caught them with their pants down. War isn't fair.

Major Bill Arther was a World War I pilot. When Pearl Harbor was bombed, he immediately requested active duty and this 43 year old retiree was accepted. What a guy. He spoke hours about his experiences in "The War to End All Wars" in air bombardment. He flew single engine planes with a bombardier in the rear open cockpit. They flew only in clear weather because instrument flying was very risky. They had a faulty air speed indicator and a six inch glass tube half filled with thick dark oil attached to the instrument panel. As they turned, glided or climbed, the pilot could understand the attitude of the plane by the shift of oil in the tube.

"What if the oil spilled out of the tube?" we asked.

"We would bail out fast, parachute wherever we were," Bill replied.

At a top speed of 105 miles an hour, they flew over enemy lines just above rifle range. The bombardier armed the 45 pound bomb on his lap and dropped it over the side.

Major Arther recruited me to take part in his intelligence work. He died in 1985 at his Vero Beach, Florida, home. I miss his stories, upbeat attitude and generous smile.

Dad seldom wrote, depending on Mother and me to keep him informed at least once every week. My first letter was a request for the Sunday comics. Within a week the first fat letter arrived, and boy, was I popular. Those papers made the rounds and never got back to me. On a mission, my crew stayed overnight at an advance base. The thick letter had arrived and my friends thought we had been shot down. They opened it, passed it around and apologized over and over when we returned. The dog-eared papers were gathered and returned with more apologies. Just writing about it makes me laugh again. We all had to read "Terry and the Pirates" by Milt Caniff. He had someone in the CBI informing him as to what we were doing and it was printed in his comic strip. At mail call, everyone checked the thickness of my letters. Mother never let us down.

Returning from a mission, we were over safe territory once we reached the Chin Hills, but we had another hour before landing at Chakulia. The sun was warm, we were relaxed, the engines were droning a lullaby, I was nodding and my copilot slugged me on the upper right arm. He shoved one of his cigars in my mouth and told me to chew it. My eyes lit up and my system jumped. I wrote mother and explained why I needed a box of cigars. She was opposed to smoking and I had never, never smoked anything. The next week two boxes of expensive cigars arrived. Crazy war. But I stayed awake.

Our beer ration arrived the first week at Chakulia—thirty cans a month for each soldier. I had never tasted beer, so I gave my ration away. The next month eighteen men formed a line at my room, offering to buy, steal, hijack, and kill for a can of beer. That did it. I thought, this must be good stuff and I turned down all offers. It turned out to be very good stuff.

The Chin Hills average 6,000 feet above sea level and are covered by steaming, thick, impassable jungle with all types of animals and poisonous snakes. To top it off, it is home to several tribes of head hunters, real sports, but there is a good side. In 1939, armed British soldiers visited them in their jungle villages and struck a deal. They were promised salt and an airplane ride for every British and U.S. soldier they rescued and brought back to India. A savage owning a few ounces of salt was very wealthy. Those guys even brought us Japs. The payoff was the same.

My first combat flight was in a five-ship mission leaving Chakulia on April 2, 1943. Each new first pilot was required to fly several times as copilot before moving to his own crew. Captain Hughes had completed 40 missions and was visibly stressed. The sky was clear; everything on the ground stood out in sharp detail from our 10,000 foot altitude and the three hour ride to Thazi, Burma, one hundred miles south of Mandalay was a piece of cake.

We dropped the bombs on a railhead and turned for home. I saw some round things floating near us and said, "Hey, Captain, look. Barrage balloons."

He gave me a withering look, turned a shade of purple, said some words bordering on Chicago gutter stuff, and ended with, "What? Balloons? THAT'S FLACK." I spent the rest of the trip gazing out the windows.

Fuel was low, so we landed at Agartela, India, near the Chin Hills for the night. The next day we again hit Thazi Junction and returned to Chakulia. That overnight saved 600 miles of flying for five B-25s. That's a lot of 100 octane gas.

Squadron commander, Captain Robert S. Puckett, wasted no time integrating new officers and sergeants in missions. On April 8, he led a nine-ship raid targeting Meiktila, twenty miles west of Thazi. I was copilot to Capt. Clarke Johnston, flying with bombardier-navigators 1st Lt. Joseph Cunningham and 2nd Lt.

Charles Brewer. S/Sgt. George Denfield was engineer-gunner and T/Sgt. John Boyd was radio-gunner. On the bombing run heading east we saw a very unusual formation. Thirty miles north of us heading west at our altitude was a flight of Japanese twin engine bombers escorted by fighters. About 1,000 yards out, a Zero followed our formation but made no attempt to attack. Our lead radio operator warned India headquarters of the impending attack. Our formation met light AA fire of heavy caliber but bursts were trailing. No B-25s were damaged and all refueled at Dum Dum before returning to Chakulia.

My fourth mission was the 78th mission for the squadron since its organization in 1942. I was copilot for 1st Lt. William Nau on a target run to the Ywataung railroad yards, a round trip mission of 6 hours 10 minutes. That's a real stretch, considering a B-25 maximum flight time is normally less than six hours before refueling. Weather was clear and an attack was made from 11,000 feet at 1005 hours with a 190-degree bomb run. Bombs of the first flight hit left of target. The second flight at 10,200 feet, had 36 direct hits on marshalling yards, destroying rolling stock, supply dumps and trackage. Large oil fires were started. AA fire of light intensity and small caliber exploded low and trailing. All nine aircraft returned with no damage or injury to the crews, but our gas tanks were knocking on empty.

On April 26, I flew with Capt. Thad Blanton on an eleven plane mission to Heho, a Jap airfield. We left Chakulia at 0320, flew the mission without incident and landed at Dum Dum at 0950. "All planes extremely low on gas upon landing," according to the flight intelligence report. One plane landed at Chittagong, out of fuel; both engines quit while taxing to the ramp. The attack on Heho began at 0645 from 15,000 feet and all bombs landed in the dispersal area. Hits were observed on Japanese planes in revetments, hangars demolished and AA positions destroyed. A single Zero approached after we left the target but did not succeed in interception. We had a good day.

All of my Burma missions were within 200 miles of Mandalay. We stayed away from that ancient Burmese Capital because of the heavy local population and the beautiful temples there. We concentrated on airfields, bridges, railroads and river traffic. Squadron mission #89 targeted the Sedow railroad reversing station on May 6, 1943. Flight Leader Captain Wilmer E. McDowell commanded a nine ship formation that attacked at 1015 from 11,000 feet. Numerous hits were observed on tracks, retaining wall and the mountainside adjacent to rail tracks. On my last mission as copilot, I again flew with Capt. Blanton. I was promoted to 1st Lt. and returned to my original crew. My baptism of fire was officially over.

Our crew on a single plane mission was ordered to look for railroad trains in the north-south valley of the Patkai Mountains bordering northwest Burma. We flew east over the Chin Hills, then south along rail tracks. The ridges of the Patkai Mountains ran parallel to the tracks, about two miles away on each side. We saw two Naga villages with thatched roof huts near the tops of two mountains. We spotted a train with nearly thirty freight cars no more than three miles ahead. We were flying at 300 feet above the ground and a solid cloud cover was beginning to form just above us. A quick glance proved that we would be flying down a tunnel region with thick clouds above us, mountains climbing into the clouds on each side, and the people running for cover below. Bombs exploded and made scrap metal out of that train. Bombardier-navigator Fred Stowers was standing beside me and pointed. "Check that," he said, "that mountain just ahead is closing off our flight path."

"How the hell do we get out of this?" I asked.

Lt. Stowers had studied his maps the day before this mission. "Turn port (left) just before that big pile of rock—port, port." So I did. It was the only opening to the Burma plain and we flew through the pass. Fred had saved our butts.

Picture yourself in a car without lights on a highway at night so black you can't see the road or any of the surrounding area. You are not sure the car is correctly lined up to drive straight ahead on that road, yet you are told to hit the gas and travel 115 miles an hour in the next ten seconds. What are your chances of success? Now let's complicate that scene. You are going on a night mission starting at 0330 down a runway with no lights on either side of the strip or lights from the aircraft because it's a secret strike. The B-25 is fully loaded with gas, bombs, and men.

You pour the coal to it, hope you started in the exact correct direction down the runway, keep your eyes on the dimly lit instrument panel and start easing back on the control column (stick) when you reach 105 miles an hour. You know tall trees grow just a few hundred feet from the end of the runway. You feel the ship leave the ground and shout to the copilot, "WHEELS," and he has the handle up before you finish the word.

Eighteen sweating pilots in nine gulls (B-25 wings are shaped like gulls) left the ground in a memorable strike. Now a new problem developed—we had to find each other to get in formation. I could see two by the light from their engine nacelles but their gulls were faster and I never joined anyone. Over the Chin Hills, as usual, everyone cleared their guns with a couple of short bursts. Tracers were visible all around us, a spectacular demonstration of possible mass suicide. My copilot refused to take his turn flying during the whole mission.

At dawn, our navigator found a target of opportunity. We bombed and headed for home. As far as I know, several others did the same thing. The Japanese probably thought the whole 10th Air Force was out to get them that morning. Your question would probably be, "When did you stop sweating?" Oh, probably two days later.

The hot dry season (85-105) in the Chakulia-Calcutta area lasts from March to June. The rainy season can last from June to September and usually the area receives heavy rain up to 102 inches. Seasonal winds called monsoons blow across the Bay of Bengal, then north over India, picking up tons of moisture on the way.

Massive clouds from 800 feet above ground level towering to 40,000 feet cover the earth for days at a time during the monsoons. The clouds always swivel and circle accompanied by severe up or down drafts. It's a severe, messy weather system that tests your skill when flying loose formation on instruments. The first ten minutes in that cauldron are sufficient, but a pilot has two hours of it toward the target and two hours returning. The balance of the time over the Chin Hills and Burma was through heavy haze. Those "under the hood" instructors back in the USA had been great. As far as I know, no aircraft were lost because of piloting through the monsoon weather. Low level instrument flying through clouds in China was a much different matter.

By October 10, 1943, those who had joined the squadron in April had completed at least 28 combat missions. Our commander gave many of us a ten-day leave.

CALCUTTA

Chakulia is 100 miles west of Calcutta, a city of six million people. Occasionally, military personnel from our base took the night train for a short vacation. Flight schedules of one combat mission a week for each rated airmen allowed us time for R&R. We probably paid ten rupees for "Executive" train fare, $3.35 U.S. Small freight cars with eight open bunks along three walls, each bunk with a three inch leather mattress was as good as it gets. Wood siding was four inches wide with half-inch spacing. Hundreds of hitchhikers clung to those boards and they stared through the small spacing for the complete five hour trip.

Yes, five hours for one hundred miles. Did we sleep? Are you serious? That Toonerville Trolley stopped at anything that seemed to be a town. It was a night time ride featuring masses of people shouting, pushing, jumping in and out of cars; train whistling, coal smoke, jarring stops, more jarring stops and then jarring starts to match. At the first stop we heard the most gut-wrenching, god-awful constant shriek you can imagine, and it didn't stop until we reached Calcutta. Hindus had captured a wild pig, tied it on a pole and were headed to market. A taxi took us to the Grand Hotel where we slept until late the next morning.

Our party of six officers had two rooms, each the size of several Holiday Inn rooms, with marble floors and walls. King size beds with mattresses had us floating on clouds. At 1300, lunchtime, four assistants (natives) served our table and no other table while we were dining. One handled silverware, china and drinks. Another supplied us with linen napkins and removed used dishes. The other two took orders in English and served food. Extraordinary. We learned how the English lived in India before the war.

Farm families by the thousands were suffering from a malaria epidemic and did not have the strength to harvest their crops. They moved to the streets of Calcutta with meager savings and looked for work that did not exist. They used their annas (pennies), begged, slept, starved and died. The English newspaper, *Hindustani Times*, printed a small box on the lower right-hand corner of the first page, numbering the bodies picked

up from the gutters by the death carts on the previous day. The daily average was 1,500.

One morning, I was walking to a gem shop less than a mile from the Grand Hotel. Beggars were sitting on the sidewalk along the route when my attention centered on an old, wisened Hindu sitting and holding a small bowl. She was probably 27 years old. I can hear her plaintive voice today. "Awa, Awa. Baksheesh, Sahib, Memsahib. Awa, Awa, Baksheesh." Over and over again, "Please, please. Give me something, Sir, Madam. Please, please, give me something."

I understood some of their language and could not take this any longer. I grabbed the arm of a young man my age, not realizing that he might have a heart attack. Americans were virtual gods to some of the people, who looked at us with a mixture of real fear and hope. Motioning with my hand to mouth as if eating, I pointed to a food shop across the street and then to the beggar. I handed him a couple of rupees (66 cents) and said, "Idder Au Jelde." (Go over there, fast.) He ran across the street, shouting to the store owner.

In record time he was back bringing cooked rice on a tray. He placed the rice in her bowl, but her dull eyes were expressionless. She kept rocking back and forth, "Awa, Awa—."

The gem shop was a small operation. The front office contained three chairs near a small coffee table in an area about eight feet square. Mr. Svedra spoke perfect "English," greeted me and motioned to a chair. We talked about everything except gems and the war for twenty minutes. At a pause, I asked to see some star sapphires. He rang a small bell and his assistant walked in carrying tea and cookies. Now he began his sales pitch. Star sapphires were very difficult to find, but he said I was fortunate because he had two of the finest. He was right. Big, nearly perfect, absolutely beautiful. I bought one for $285 U.S., which I lost a week later. It is now the year 2001 and the price is over $10,000.

"Are you doing anything for those people dying on the streets?" I asked. "Surely you should do something to help them."

He reacted, surprised. "You obviously do not understand. If my next door neighbor or best friend were starving I would not help them. They are very fine people and in their next lives on this earth they will return in much better circumstances."

How do you argue with that religion? I returned to the hotel, passing the area once occupied by the lady with the small piece of cloth she used for a dress. She had died and was pushed into the gutter. Someone had taken her bowl of rice. A cart would pick her up that evening and she would be a statistic in the *Hindustani Times* the next day.

Starving Hindus stood in a line as wide as the sidewalk extending for a block toward the rear of the Grand Hotel.

Curious, we checked this out. The hotel had hired two men who scooped a handful from the large garbage cans and gave it to the ones in line. No "seconds."

Every trip to Calcutta was a new adventure. We stayed at the Grand Hotel because it was clean, modern and had real bathrooms with sinks, showers and toilets—a rare circumstance. Most hotels had a v-shaped, four-inch deep trench along the concrete hall, ending at a hole extending to the ground where the human waste was picked up and carted to farms for fertilizer.

The first floor of the Grand Hotel boasted a large central ballroom with tables for 150 guests. A balcony twelve feet above the main floor circled the ballroom and was connected by stairways. Perhaps 150 could be served there. U.S. and British officers gathered after 1600 for a drink before dinner. The British preferred the balcony. We had tried mixing several times but the British always sniffed about "you colonials" or, "Really chaps, you seem an underclass sort." Those were the nice comments. They also let us know we were "over paid, over sexed and over there." True, our pay was three times their pay, we probably were over sexed and we absolutely were over there. They were jealous and we let it pass. But not tonight.

The evening began quietly, but within an hour a few taunts were hurled from our British friends in the balcony. After an interval, a U.S. officer shouted an insult that carried to the whole balcony. A breathless silence on both sides threatened like the eye of a hurricane. A glass from the balcony smashed on a table-top. More glasses, then a chair, and the place erupted with a roar. It was a satisfactory fight as the Brits came down the stairways.

MPs blocked the exits and colonels of each army stopped the fighting. Our colonel said we would pay for the damage because we were guests of the British colonial empire. We were and we did. Then we invited the Brits to have a couple of drinks on our tab. Thus ended the second Revolutionary War. This time it was a draw. No reports were filed.

Tourist attractions in Calcutta are just one big surprise after another. One October afternoon I hired a taxi to "show me the city." Two muscular, bearded Sikhs occupied the front seats of a 1930 open canopy, English sedan that had seen better days. Much better. Off we went around Chowringee Square, horn blaring and my guides shouting at everyone within foghorn range. Hundreds of people were either pulling carts, rushing in different directions, or just standing in groups talking and screaming. Some would grab the side of our slow moving car, yell and shake their fists for no apparent reason. The back seat was mine and I felt secure with a shoulder holster and pistol covered by a leather flight jacket.

Our first stop was an open air market, one of several hundred "grocery stores." The market was two blocks long on a narrow walking street with twenty-foot wide food booths packed on each side. I walked into that human maelstrom and looked at perhaps eight booths before forcing my way back to the taxi. What I had seen were flies. Each shopkeeper had a whisk broom that he waved over his produce. That gave a quick look at what he was selling before the voracious flies settled back for dinner. Flies were at least three deep, each forcing their way to the meat, rice or other vegetables.

Our next stop on this delightful, fun-filled afternoon was an open air church enclosed by a bamboo lattice fence. Three swaying, half naked priests and an altar with a goat tied on top filled a quarter of the "church." A dozen chosen beggars crouched in one open area, chanting and slapping their hands on the dirt floor. Priests made it clear that as a spectator to this most important sacrifice, I was expected to drop ten rupees into an extended bowl. Some of those rupees probably went to my guides. The ritual began with chanting, hand and body movement, then the quick swing of a sharp machete that cut off the goat's head. It was thrown to the beggars who fondled it and rubbed some of the blood on their torso. Two of the men plucked the eyes and ate them. I presume they cooked the head and the rest of the goat was prepared for the priests. I don't know because I left one second after the eye gouging incident. You shouldn't be reading this while having breakfast, lunch or dinner, or even a light snack.

Things tamed down a bit at the burning ghats along the Hooghly River. Bodies were burned on layered piles of wood and the ashes were later pushed into the river. A few yards downstream and extending for a mile south, Hindus were taking their religious baths.

My guides said that we had time for one more viewing and what would I like to do. My immediate reaction was what could be done to spoil a perfectly distressing afternoon? I had enough of this stuff and these Sikhs, so, "Take me to an ice cream store." Big surprise. It was the only one in this city of six million and the ice "cream" was made from water buffalo milk. You chew it to break down the lumps. It was now evening and I asked them to take me to the famed Coffee House near the Grand Hotel. Again, off we drove with horn blaring. I could see more trouble ahead because we were not heading toward Chowringee Road.

Those Sikhs pulled onto a quiet street, got out on each side of the car, opened the doors to the back seat and stopped, staring at me. I was sitting in the center, holding my pistol with both hands, ready to shoot the first wild man who even thought of making an aggressive move. They backed off, climbed into the front, never looked back, drove me to the Coffee House and politely opened the door for me. I got out and walked into the Coffee House where I met some friends. The Sikhs drove away. They never received a rupee for the afternoon. The Devil must have practiced his trade in Calcutta before he created Hell.

MORE ABOUT DARJEELING

I recall the Sunday concert at the small Darjeeling park. A proud and "exclusive" corps of Ghurka soldiers wearing perfectly tailored, authentic Scotsman kilts played bagpipes for an hour while strolling. Gurkhas average four feet ten inches tall. They are very strong and carry wicked two-foot long chopping knives that slice through bamboo or necks with one stroke. No man is a match in a close fight.

The local club was called Gymkhana, a two-room affair. Elmer, Steve and I were in the bar and discovered that a couple of drinks at that altitude were much more than enough.

Dancing in the next room was roaring along, shaking the floor. Steve shouted, "Cut out the racket," and suddenly everything became perfectly quiet.

We congratulated him. The next morning our Ghurka bearer mentioned that no one was killed in last night's earthquake. Two drinks and we could not tell the difference between dancing and a major earth tremor.

We wore our Class A uniforms with blouse and tie three times up there in the clouds. We had not worn them since leaving the U.S. and we did not wear them again until we returned to the

U.S. Three days out of 390. Why were we ordered to take them to combat operations? What a waste. It's a war, stupid.

YANGKAI, CHINA

Everything had to be moved by air from the province of Assam in northeast India over the "Hump" to our new base at Yangkai, China, deep in the interior and very close to the Himalaya Mountain range.

The "Hump" has north to south mountain ridges up to 17,000 feet with steep sides dropping down to white water rivers far below. Planes flew through mountain passes, where possible, at 14,000 feet and at times at their maximum rated altitude. "Hump" pilots and their C-46 or C-47 transport planes carried loads of our supplies over that treacherous 500 mile trip. Down drafts could suck a plane 2,000 feet in a matter of seconds. Slowly, it would regain altitude and continue on to Yangkai. Jap Zeros flew north from Burma and occasionally shot them down. No rescue was possible in that extremely rugged terrain. "Hump" cargo planes had a greater loss percentage than most combat groups throughout the world.

On January 10, 1944, we left Chakulia for the last time, flying northeast to Chabua, a small landing strip in Assam province. Ten miles west of Chabua is Dibrugarh, a major city by the Brahmaputra River. We waited for the weather over the "Hump" to clear. Our crew was joined by a major who had flown the route many times. I flew as copilot and had one of the most hair-raising times of my career.

The B-25 bucked like a wild bronco and strained its guts to maintain altitude. We had one 1,800 foot down draft that dropped us between peaks in the Qingshuilang Shan range of the lower Himalayas. It took 45 minutes to squeeze between a couple of peaks. I glanced at the major several times, but we never spoke. He had that tight, grim look of a man fighting for our lives. I have relived that experience several times.

September, 1941, to January, 1944, seemed like a minute in time but a century of life and death. Landing at Yangkai caused me to stop and think about the violence and massive destruction I had been a part of during this short time. Four roommates from the four training bases had died. Cadet Carl Larson spun out at Rankin Field in Tulare, California, during his seventh solo flight. Lt. Munns was lost in combat over Germany. Lt. Hollemen from San Antonio crashed in Italy. Lt. Barton's B25 exploded 500 feet over Greenville, South Carolina, scattering parts over 30 acres.

Four days after arriving in Chakulia, word reached us that thirty six officers and airmen we had replaced were killed on their way home. Their commercial C-54 left Accra on the Gold Coast of Africa and crashed twenty minutes later over the South

Atlantic—thirty six brothers who had completed fifty combat missions. Several 22nd Bomb Squadron gulls (B-25s were equipped with gull wings) had been lost on Burma strikes. They gave their best; they gave everything. Sure, I know millions of people were killed in World War II, killed or wounded, but it is the guy in the next bunk, the guy that you played softball with, the guys that you flew with, those are the men you grieve for. I salute you, Brothers.

One of my copilots who eventually became a first pilot remembers the geographic details of Yangkai. Lt. Jesse "Chuck" Weber writes:

The base at Yangkai was located about 45 miles north east of Kunming, province of Yunnan in China. It was located in a fairly broad valley with a field elevation of 6,426' MSL. (This compares to Cheyenne, Wyoming, at 6,115', Colorado Springs at 6,300', Denver at 5,330' and Salt Lake City of 6,440' MSL.) This high field elevation caused reduced power from all engines (particularly noticeable in aircraft), reduced efficiency from both wings and propellers. The runway was oriented NE-SW, this resulting in our flying the downwind leg at 8,500' to maintain 600 to 800 feet of terrain clearance. There was another parallel ridge to the west and, within 25 miles, peaks at 9,000 to 10,000 MSL.

The control tower was located on the west side of the runway as were the 'alert' shack and other supporting structures. Other peripheral facilities, fuel and ammo dumps, firing range and the 491st Bomb Squadron's flight line were on the east side of the runway. Barracks and other personnel facilities were located on the west side of the valley, nestled against the ridge paralleling the runway.

The two areas were connected by an unsmooth dirt/gravel road, which divided various low-lying fields that were surrounded by earthen mounds/walls. Rice appeared to be the predominant crop. Like most fields in China, they were fertilized with human manure called night soil. On the road on many occasions, I observed many bullock carts that were used for hauling stone. The walled bed was about three and one-half feet by five feet and the cart had solid wooden wheels about 30 inches square with the corners rounded. Those carts were the subject of ridicule until we realized that, without brakes, those wheels effectively controlled speed on the down slopes in this hilly terrain.

The barracks, and particularly the officer barracks, represented the best available construction in that part of China. The foundations and interior floors were concrete, the walls were stucco, and the roofs were terra-cotta tile. The window frames and sashes were wood with glass panes, mostly. The secondary buildings had oiled paper for panes. They were heated with pot-bellied, coal-fired stoves.

The native housing, however, was of home-made mud bricks (mud mixed with straw) and tile roofs, mud floors and streets.

It was not uncommon to see mature women whose feet were not more than four to five inches long. Their feet had been bound since birth in an effort to duplicate the small feet of a princess who was regarded as very beautiful.

I believe that Jesse "Chuck" Weber was a meticulous observer of everything. He gave me these observations just months before his death in 1999. Chuck was an airline pilot until his retirement and wrote many pages of his experiences while a commercial pilot.

FLYING MISSIONS IN CHINA

I flew 42 combat missions from India over Burma. After the first 26, there was a change in crew personnel. Lt. Parkhurst, previously my copilot, was promoted to first pilot with a new crew and Sgt. Napoleon Plante was assigned tail gunner on Lt. T.J. Smith's crew. My crew had flown one low altitude mission (under 300 feet) over Burma. In China, B-25 crews flew mainly low altitude missions and were subject to all types of enemy gunfire and foul weather.

Our first missions were bridge busting along railroads a few miles inland from the China coast. Search and destroy was the order, so off we went into the wild blue yonder in three-ship flights at tree top level, searching for a railroad and following it to a bridge. There were plenty of bridges. We would begin an attack three miles from a bridge, the bomb sight aiming for the foundation on the far side. Bomb bay doors were open and, when necessary, all stations were firing 50 caliber machine guns. A single bomb would be dropped, and if aimed correctly it exploded under the far end of the bridge. If the first missed, the other two B-25 crews would take their turn. Very effective.

Three B-25s were flying at treetop level following a river, looking for bridges, when ground fire struck the pilot in the lead

ship. Lt. T.J. Smith must have fallen forward on the control column and the plane dove, plowing into the river bottom. A tip of the tail section remained above water. At 170 miles an hour, all five, including tail gunner Sgt. Napoleon Plante, were instantly killed.

In February, 1944, we began flying missions to the Gulf of Tonkin off the coast of China and French Indochina, now known as Vietnam. Cloud cover at times extended from below mountains to 40,000 feet. We flew on instruments and then let down over the Gulf. Colonel Weatherly returned from one of those missions and found me in the ready room.

"Hanson," he said, "we never got to the gulf. We didn't realize a strong head wind was blowing and we let down too soon, right among the mountains. My wingman, Doc Parkhurst, must have hit one. I could see mountains at my wingtips all the way up to safe altitude. I am very sorry for your loss and I will write to his wife. I know he was married shortly before shipping out. Please take care of his locker and financials." Doc had thousands of Chinese dollars, which he had purchased at the black market rate of 200 for one American dollar. If you left China alive, that would be your exchange rate. If you died, the U.S. allowed the official rate of 20 to 1, a gain of ten times the original amount of U.S. dollars. Doc had exchanged nearly $350 for $7,000 Chinese. I sent his widow $3,500 U.S. and his personal items. She also received his G.I. insurance of $10,000. The $13,500 would translate into $128,000 in today's market. Clothing and anything useful in the war effort was used by the squadron. Doc never frowned. That man from Arkansas had a smile and a good word for everyone. The son he never saw lives in the Carolinas.

On one mission we were ordered to find cargo ships and rattle their cage. My copilot said, "Hey, look ahead, a submarine." We knew no allied subs were in the area so, "Bomb bay doors open"—just two minutes ahead, pure excitement. We looked again and saw a submarine shaped rock. "Bomb bay doors

closed." We never mentioned it in our report but word got around. One wise guy suggested we get the Navy Double Cross.

The B-25H model featuring a 75 mm cannon arrived in January. The barrel stuck out the nose and extended back to a small compartment below and behind the pilot seat. The navigator added the name "cannoneer" to his title, loading the shells for the pilot to fire. No guidelines were issued as to type of targets. Perhaps bridges? I tried that and nothing seemed to happen. The fourth shot went high over the bridge and struck a three story building, folding it into match sticks. So, we shot at buildings until we switched to shipping. What a gas.

A big fishing hole was Haiphong Harbor, fifty miles east of Hanoi. The Japs were filling every type of ship with raw materials from French Indochina (Vietnam) and taking the booty to Japan. The 75 mm cannons blew a lot of holes in ships; bombs and machine guns did their share.

Officers I knew in China told me the following story. They admitted no actual witnesses could be found so let's call it a strong rumor.

Soldiers were at the flight line, watching planes return from a combat mission to the South China Sea. Flames poured out of its starboard engine, wheels and flaps were damaged. A B-25 crashed and came to a screeching halt. Everyone used escape hatch exits except the flight engineer, crouched behind the pilot's seat. Flames shot up from broken fuel lines and roared into the cockpit, covering him. "My foot is trapped, I can't get out," the sergeant shouted.

Everyone ran toward the plane but stopped twenty feet short of the wing because of the searing heat. "Shoot me, shoot me, my God, the pain," he shouted. A major hesitated, then aimed his pistol and emptied it, scoring direct hits. The sergeant was quiet.

Of course, there was a courts martial. The decision was announced ten minutes after all testimony was reviewed. The major was acquitted. The court concluded that the sergeant died in the fire one second before the bullets hit him.

I had met many people on three continents. Those I learned to respect and admire were the town dwellers and farmers of interior China. They were sincere, honest, and helpful unto death. A heavily damaged B-25 was forced to ditch (crash land) in enemy territory. Chinese peasants passed the airmen from village to village, returning them to Kunming. We were told that Japanese soldiers killed every man, woman and child in the village near the crash site. The Chinese continued to help us, however.

TIME TO RELAX

Kunming, a large city, was a one hour Jeep ride from Yangkai, and occasionally we drove to the shopping area and Billy's Café. One afternoon I was lost, stopped on a street corner, and waited for any soldier who could tell me where Billy's Café was located. No luck. A small crowd of Chinese gathered and I smiled, spoke English, and asked for directions. They laughed, spoke their dialect and waited for something to happen. The crowd grew to over a hundred happy people. This attracted the attention of a very old Chinaman who spoke perfect English. I told him my problem and the crowd shouted, asking what I wanted. When he told them, all hands shot in the air, everyone wanted to walk with me to Billy's Café.

He chose a couple my age. The father carried their year old son and we went smiling on our way. They knew the best stores to visit and I purchased some baby clothes that I shipped to Sioux Falls. The cape is brightly colored and the little red cap has a four inch string attached at the peak. If the baby were to die, the powers that be would use this string to pull it to heaven. At the café, I removed a bundle ($1500) of Chinese money ($7.50 U.S.) from my jacket as a tip. They froze. My mistake. Offering them money for their kindness was highly insulting. Without pausing, I put it in the hands of the baby boy, a present for him. His parents relaxed and the smiles broke out again. I had honored their child and we departed as friends.

Weatherly was promoted to "bird" colonel long after he returned to the ZI (zone of the interior—USA). He was a major when I knew him in India and China, but I think of him as a great commander and shall continue to use the title colonel when referring to him.

Colonel Weatherly, Captain Tom Carey and I had a day clear of any detail work so we decided it was time to go hunting. It

193

took ten minutes to check pistols, fix some cheese sandwiches and gas up a Jeep. We drove northeast on a dirt road for eight miles into a high valley between towering mountains. We stopped at a roadside inn that featured a couple of open air tables and benches. More than 25 curious Chinese gathered to watch our every move or mood. From the way they reacted to our faces and clothing, I doubt most had ever seen a "westerner." We purchased delicious tea served in small round bowls and opened our stock of cheese sandwiches.

Surprised, they all talked at once, pointing at the sandwiches. Then, complete silence as we began eating. We offered small bites of one sandwich to most of those friendly people who promptly began chewing. Within two seconds all had gagged, spit the bread and cheese pieces on the ground, coughed, grimaced and spit some more.

They watched closely as we finished our lunch, no doubt commenting all the time about the vile food we ate with their great tea. Crazy Americans.

We drove a couple of miles and stopped in the middle of nowhere. We spaced ourselves about 200 feet and began walking up a gradual slope. Within half an hour, Tom and I heard a shot and walked over to Colonel Weatherly. He had seen the eyes of an animal sheltered under a huge rock and shot it. Its size, shape and tail puzzled us and we returned to Yangkai with the trophy.

No one could identify the creature, so it was flown to India on one of the regular flights, with a request for help. We never received any information. I had taken a few pictures of that safari and brought them back on rotation to the ZI (zone of the interior).

The animal is identified as Mallaccensis, or the "Small Indian Civet," a ground dweller that sometimes uses its sharp claws to climb trees. It has a very narrow head, relatively large ears, sharper claws than other civets and lacks a dorsal mane. The species is distributed throughout central and southern Asia and China.

In Kunming, I was seated at a banquet next to a Chinese general when he let loose with a belch that shook the room. It scared my socks off. Later I learned the louder the belch the higher the compliment to those in charge. Try that in Washington, DC, sometime.

As to their rice wine, don't drink it. Smooth, oh so smooth and higher than high point. Shortly after arriving at Yangkai our flight surgeon, Captain Leslie L. Daviet, asked five of us to do "straight jacket" duty. An airman with too much wine had turned mean and wild. It took all of us to get him in that jacket. The jail for this type of offense was his own bunk. When he passed out, we took off the jacket and his friends handled things for the rest of the night.

A round table in the officers' club was occupied by four lieutenants sipping smooth rice wine that creates a sense of overrated intelligence. At about 2100 hours, one well-oiled lieutenant had an idea and said, "Let's go to Kunming." No one had ever done this without the colonel's permission, but it sounded O.K. to that bunch of happy warriors. Another said, "Let's borrow the colonel's Jeep, he won't miss it."

That settled it. Forty-five minutes down that hilly, winding, dirt and gravel road they made a sharp turn, tipping the Jeep on its side and spilling them into a slow moving, five foot deep river. All except Jim. He landed in some brush beside the river, half knocked out. The other three came up sputtering, counted noses, and figured Jim was still in the water. They waded ashore, removed all of their clothes and went back in looking for Jim. Meanwhile, Jim wobbled to his feet, saw everyone shouting and swimming, took off his clothes and joined them. Not too much later the conversation went something like this:

Jim asked, "What are we looking for?"

"We're looking for Jim."

Surprised, Jim said, "I'm Jim."

They counted heads that moonlit night and discovered they were all back together.

Meanwhile, many Chinese pedestrians had walked by on the road and when our heroes sloshed out of the river, all their clothes had disappeared. That started to sober them up. What to do? Those naked jaybirds began walking that dirt and gravel road toward Kunming. A truckload of Chinese soldiers stopped, spoke Chinese and moved on, shaking their heads. Those crazy Americans. Then two sergeants in a Jeep stopped. Laughing hysterically, they piled the lieutenants into their Jeep and drove to Kunming.

At Yangkai the next morning, Colonel Weatherly was furious. Where is my Jeep? Where are those officers? Put them on report. Courts martial them. Boil them in oil. The story of the sorry four and the rage of the colonel went all the way up to

General Chennault. He solved it in a few minutes. A letter was placed in Weatherly's 201 file, praising him for his duty time in China. Orders were cut for his return to the ZI. The lieutenants were returned to duty with a mild reprimand, not to be included in their permanent file. General Chennault needed them more than the good colonel. And let that be a lesson to all good colonels.

CHIANG MAI, THAILAND

All the skills we had developed were needed and expertly used on my 50th and last combat mission. On the morning of March 5, 1944, at 0800 I was ordered to report immediately to Colonel Edison C. Weatherly, squadron commander. His office was a hundred feet from my barracks and I got there before the orderly who brought the message. Weatherly, group intelligence officer Major Arther and squadron operations officer Captain Jerry D. Miller were waiting. Major Arther said, "General Chennault has information from intelligence sources that Japanese fighters and bombers are assembling at the Chiang Mai air field together with five to seven thousand combat engineers and riflemen stationed there. They are probably planning to strike at 14th Air Force installations."

"Lt. Hanson," Captain Miller continued, "your crew will take the lead on this mission.

"We will assemble planes and crews for takeoff today. Chiang Mai is 500 plus miles to the south, in a large valley. The mission may extend beyond the point of no return."

I frowned, thought, and slowly rubbed my chin. Beyond the point of no return? That may mean we haven't enough gas to get back and we have never been placed in that position before. He must mean that we will use our reserve ten minutes of fuel and we had better find that air field straight on. I asked Colonel Weatherly about his assessment of the possible fuel problem.

"General Chennault worked that out with his engineering officer," Weatherly said. "If you lean the fuel mixture, have no crosswinds and use Kunming air field on the return flight, there should be no problem. Milk it for all it's worth, Hanson, we did it over Burma."

Suddenly the poem, "Charge of the Light Brigade" by Alfred Lord Tennyson (1809–1892) struck me like a thunderbolt.

Different war (India), different century, a cavalry attack–but the issue was similar:

> Theirs was not to make reply,
> Theirs was not to reason why,
> Theirs was but to do and die;
> Into the Valley of Death
> Rode the Six Hundred.

I changed the last line to:

Rode the Forty-Five Flying Tigers.

The gravity of the mission began to sink in. We had never organized a mission in less than two days. If we failed to surprise the enemy, the attack would end like Custer's at Little Big Horn. We had no fighter escort. "General Chennault has ordered a pre-emptive strike," Major Arther explained. "He has issued a series of directives and the most important states  that you are to attack at low level—300 feet—at dusk and fly back after dark. He believes any Jap Zero getting off the ground can't find and attack you."

The initial briefing concluded at 0845 and we had a ton of work to do and very few hours before takeoff in our nine-ship formation. By 0900, Base Operations moved smoothly and swiftly; there was no room for error. Orders were issued in every direction. Captain Miller checked the number of operational Gulls available. By 1300, three B-25H models with twelve .50 caliber machine guns and a 75 mm cannon, plus three B-25C models were ready at the 22nd Bomb Squadron. Three B-25Cs were added by the 491st Bomb Squadron.

The Armament section loaded parafrags with butterfly fuses. These bombs were small, weighing less than 25 pounds, eight bundled together. Released from a bomb bay the bundles would immediately open, allowing the bombs to strike the target area in trail. Designed for attack under 500 feet altitude, the bombs had small parachutes that would swing them nose-down. The butterfly fuse was a disk two inches in diameter that activated an explosion when deflected by the slightest impact—a leaf, twig or grass. The bomb was designed as an air burst against aircraft and personnel.

Nine ships carried a total of at least 800 parafrags, adequate for this low level attack. All were expected to be direct hits at our assigned bombing altitude–300 feet. Several belts of .50 caliber machine gun bullets were stowed aboard each gull, together with 75mm shells for the H models. The navigator would load the cannon and notify the pilot when it was ready to be fired. Our "high tech" communication method in those days was swift and sure. The navigator hit the pilot's shoulder with a three foot long stick. A pilot could tell how excited the navigator was by the strength of the whack.

Meteorologists gave us a mixed bag by 1400. Scattered clouds existed going south, and cloud cover in and over mountains would be found on the way back. Tropical Chiang Mai would be hot, hot, hot, and very humid. Returning, we would be forced to fly over the clouds by the light of the moon, or by the homing device at Kunming or, if that didn't work—by dead reckoning or star triangulation. "Wow," I said to myself, "On the way south, fly between mountain ridges and then slide into the I.P. (initial point of the sighted bombing run), after several hours of uncharted jungle. My navigator Lt. Jay Percival is a magician, but this???"

Navigators were working on precision timing of takeoff, distance, air speed and ground speed, climate change and scheduled arrival time at the I.P. Climate change was important. We would fly southerly from 25 degrees latitude to 18.40 degrees, deep in the tropics. Pilots needed to carry large rags to wipe the sweat out of their eyes. Flying that same distance is similar to a trip from Laredo, Texas, to Mexico City.

Mechanics and flight engineers checked every inch of the gulls, assuring perfect flying conditions. Failure to take off because of engine problems would be a huge black mark on the ship's mechanics. The chief mechanic for each plane was the flight engineer with the combat crew.

Lt. Jesse C. Weber, a former copilot of my crew, was now a first pilot. During the conference with all personnel before takeoff, he remarked, "Of course, we all know a B-25 operates easily from a 4,000 foot runway at sea level, but this Yangkai runway on a warm spring day at 6,420 feet altitude is a different matter. Let's use every foot available on the runway." Good advice.

Navigator Jay Percival did a masterful job of dead reckoning above that uncharted jungle as we flew between mountain ridges. He crouched beside me, giving changes in headings sometimes as small as one degree. None of us had ever flown SSW (south-southwest) to Chiang Mai, 500 miles into enemy territory. Sweat time was ahead.

After three plus hours Jay said, "Hanson, I see your altimeter shows 5,000 feet altitude. On this heading, start descending to 400 feet. I don't know MSL (mean sea level) at the base of this narrow valley, so it's your judgment. In a few minutes I will suggest you bank to 180 degrees starboard, around that mountain just ahead and the target should be directly in front of us."

He did and it was breathtaking. It is still difficult to believe a mere human could navigate that well with what we had to work with in 1944. A broad plain extending south for several miles opened before our eyes. Five miles ahead in that green valley, steaming in the evening heat, lay the north-south runway of Chiang Mai air field. We were lined up on the runway at about 300 feet altitude, as if to land. Zeros were parked everywhere. Betty twin engine bombers were parked in revetments. On the far side, we saw all types of buildings under a grove of large shade trees. We had completely surprised them.

It took only a second to observe what lay before us. Our B-25s spread out on each side of the lead ship as we dropped to 200 feet. Several thousand Japanese soldiers would be ready with their rifles. The shooting for them and for our guns was perfect. We had two minutes before we reached the north end of their runway, then one minute (two and one half miles) over the airfield and building area, then a climbing 180 degree turn back over the airfield. All this was in our minds as we began the bombing-strafing runs. All personnel were at their stations, ready to fire the 50's. Pilots controlled the firing of 75 mm cannons and twin 50's on each side of the nose. The navigators had loaded the cannons before we saw the airfield. We were a small war armada ready to strike.

The B-25H model did not have copilots, which made my job complicated. In sequence, I fired the cannon, opened the bomb bay doors, fired two bursts from the machine guns, and Jay struck me on the shoulder. I released the bomb clusters, shot two more machine gun bursts and fired the cannon again while flying the Gull. We were now over the middle of their air field and the balance of the bombs were released in trail. The crew continued to fire machine gun bursts out the sides, to the rear and from the turret just above and behind the pilot. Six forward firing guns were controlled by a button on the pilot's control column. Gulls shook and sounded as if bombs were exploding inside their planes. Cannon fire loosened rivets. The bombs were released and the bomb bay doors were closed.

We made a climbing 180 degree turn back over their complex, now charging north over the same area. This time I nailed a Jap Betty twin engine bomber in a revetment, a three sided mound of earth built for protection. We were so close on the pullout that we flew only 50 feet above the ground and directly through the exploding debris. I wondered why Jay had not struck my shoulder after loading the third 75 mm shell. Thirty-nine years later I met Jay in Seattle during a Squadron reunion and he told me his story.

A large rag helped wipe the sweat from my eyes. The oppressive heat and humidity caused sweat to soak my body. Did those thousands of Jap riflemen take some of us out? There was no way of determining how many gulls were following as we left Chiang Mai and began climbing to 10,000 feet to be over the mountains and clouds.

If my condition was any criteria, every crewman was physically and mentally exhausted. Lt. Jay Percival and I had several more hours of navigation and flying time while the others relaxed. No Zeros seemed to have followed. They didn't know where we were from or where we were going. The Japs were caught by surprise and most of their planes were damaged or blown to pieces.

So off we flew into the wild dark yonder—and flew and flew some more. Jay kept giving me minor degree changes as he "shot" the stars, or whatever the hell he was doing. Solid, smooth clouds covered the earth like a blanket of snow just 300 feet below. Pale moonlight was not much comfort. I was plenty worried. With no copilot to relieve me for even twenty minutes I was beginning to lose concentration. Fatigue and stress were always a danger in every mission.

Enemy fire had ruined the instrument lights. A tiny flashlight held in my right hand flicked from instrument to controls to many more instruments in a constant movement. Probably youth and adrenaline kept me alert. The radio was badly damaged, fuel tanks were very low, hydraulic lines were broken and fluid was all over the floor, and we could not contact radio-gunner Jesse G. Spencer or photographer-gunner Clarence E. Strike in the aft compartment. Were they wounded or dead? What was the condition of the aircraft back there? As for Jay, it was a long haul over unknown mountainous terrain at night and he had only the stars to work with.

It was a tense, lousy three hours.

The gas gauges were banging on empty when Jay tapped me on the right shoulder, pointed down, and close to my right ear he spoke the magic word: "KUNMING."

In a few seconds—more big trouble—A small hole in the clouds revealed the city lights. The gull responded to the controls and did a partial wing over, and we dove through that opening. There were a few seconds of vertigo as I focused on the vast panorama of lights below. Lt. Jay Percival had done it again. That magician saved our lives. I radioed the tower, "Gull number seven one, landing on runway 270." No response. I asked radio operator Jesse G. Spencer to contact the tower. Immediately he said on the intercom, "Lieutenant, my equipment is all shot up. No way can we contact K-Radio." What else could happen, I wondered?

I lined up on the runway and tried to lever the wheels and flaps down. Nothing happened. Flight engineer Sgt. Jones had warned me as we left Chiang Mai that hydraulic lines were broken and fluid was all over the basic floor. He shouted, "Go around again. I'll get the wheels down mechanically."

"The gas gauge shows empty," I replied.

"Piss in the gas tank sir, you'll have enough gas," he replied. That guy didn't want to land wheels up and neither did I. It would be my third crash landing and at the moment I wasn't quite up to it. So I pushed the throttles wide open and the engines caught with a roar. We climbed, banking left through the blackness of night, on instruments. My full concentration was on that instrument panel.

In that maneuver it was vitally necessary to maintain at least a 15 degree bank and 180 degree turn. Anything less and we would strike a mountain just south of Kunming. This time we lined up ten miles from the runway, ready to land. Sgt. Jones shouted "Can't get the wheels down. No flaps."

I pressed the intercom and said, "Emergency. Blow the exits. Crash landing."

Emergency doors just above and behind my head and another in the rear compartment located near the radio operator and tail gunner blew off. A roar of air filled our plane. Jay announced our arrival by shooting a 'very' pistol that sent a sparkling shower of flame through the escape hatch. At least, Kunming now knew we were in a lot of trouble.

We landed with a sickening jar that about broke my tailbone. There was nothing I could do but hold on until the earthquake we were riding would stop jarring us into jelly. My head snapped forward on impact and then slowly swiveled until it ended on the headrest as the plane slid to a halt, facing the way we had approached. It had done a perfect 180 degree turn on the runway.

I looked out the windows and saw heavy dust, smoke and flicks of light. Fire! Percival and Jones dove out the top escape hatch, and then I got out and sat on top of that destroyed gull. No fire. The landing lights had flickered through the dust clouds and the effect had convinced me that the plane was on fire. Crew members were near the starboard wing dancing, shouting, laughing and jumping up and down. All except Lt. Jay Percival. He was running toward the operations building as if all the devils of Hell were after him. The next time I saw Jay was in Seattle, 1993, during a 22nd Bomb Squadron Association reunion. His

exceptionally good looking son, now older than when I had last seen Jay, was with him.

I don't recall flying a B-25D model to Yangkai the next day, but my flight log lists 30 minutes of daytime combat time. Japanese bombers must have been around somewhere. That 50th mission was a real blast and everyone was giving me time to rest. After a week, Colonel Weatherly offered me the position of squadron operations officer. I declined with thanks and said, "Colonel, that last mission used up all the luck I had in reserve." The mechanics at Kunming said there were so  many bullet holes in our gulls that everyone deserved the Purple Heart medal. But not one airman of the 22nd was even scratched.

Unfortunately, the 491st had lost one plane and crew. Weatherly showed me pictures confirming the immense damage at Chiang Mai.

A letter arrived from General Chennault for my personnel file and with it the Distinguished Flying Cross and a second Air Medal. Orders promoting me to Captain arrived the next day. Later, the Chinese Government sent me a commendation Medal for Victory.

In the first week of April, 1944, a cargo plane flew me over the Hump to India and C-54's returned me to Florida, zone of the interior. Home.

TO THOSE WHO MADE IT HOME, AND TO THOSE WE LEFT BEHIND, GOD BLESS EACH AND EVERY ONE OF YOU IN THAT BROTHERHOOD OF WORLD WAR II.

Jay V. Percival
MY RECOLLECTION

I remember well the day in 1944 when we raided the Japanese base at Chiang Mai, Thailand. We were the lead plane of nine, loaded with parafrags. We came in at treetop level and got most of their planes in the revetments on the first pass. That's when we should have started for home. Instead, we circled above the base firing the cannon and 50 caliber machine guns. I remember the cannon got hot after about three rounds and the last shell I tried to put in jammed halfway and we had to fly back that way.

We got hit with a 20 mm anti-aircraft shell that ruptured the hydraulic system. It also came through the back of the aluminum cannoneer's seat where I had been sitting. The only reason I wasn't hit was that I was standing to take another 75 mm shell out of the rack to reload the cannon. It was then that I noticed the pink hydraulic fluid on the floor where I was standing.

On the flight back, we had complications. We got separated from the others. It was very dark and cloudy. The cockpit was dark and we couldn't see the instruments except when Hanson shined a little handheld light. Navigation was difficult because it was impossible to hold airspeed and course steady and it was too dark to see the ground below. When we were almost out of gas and our ETA (estimated time of arrival) was up, we spotted a tiny light below in an opening in the clouds. It was Kunming. The

209

wheels wouldn't go all the way down and the flaps wouldn't work because of the hydraulic leak. We had to land immediately because we were practically out of gas. Wendell Hanson did a masterful job of bringing it in with the wheels dangling, for a belly landing.

William H. Van Vleck
AS I REMEMBER IT

During June, July and August of 1944, the weather was unfit for flying, so most of our time was spent maintaining equipment, getting sack time and playing cards. Our barracks had a continuous cribbage game in progress, with the players changing occasionally. We played for a penny a hole, with two cents per hole for a skunk. Some of us won quite a few pennies by the time we were rotated to Uncle Sugar. When the weather was not too prohibitive there were baseball and football games to keep us out of trouble.

During October, when the weather improved, Merrill's Marauders began their southward march through Burma, clearing out Japanese installations that had been harassing our supply routes into China. The jungle was so dense along much of their path that it was impractical to move heavy artillery with them; therefore, the 22nd Bomb Squadron was assigned the task of bombing and strafing the targets, which he requested. We would skip-bomb the target in the morning, then proceed to 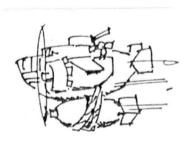 Chabua, Assam, where we refueled and loaded more bombs for an attack on the target again on the return flight to Yangkai in the afternoon.

Whenever Louis Dorn, our radio operator, received a radio plot of enemy aircraft looking for us, we would descend to treetop altitude and outrun it. Enemy ground fire was encountered on all targets, but as we were skip bombing there was no ack-ack seen, and damage and casualties were light.

211

It was during these missions when someone got the idea of taking eggs with us in the morning, trading them for good bread (at least better than the Chinese bread) which we brought back in the afternoon—hence the term "egg runs." Soon the bread was changed to beer (of which we had none), and that was enjoyed more. A B-25 with its limited unused space presented a problem, so we loaded the crawl space between the bombardier's compartment and the front hatch, also on the aft radio compartment hatch and photo hatch. One afternoon, a bombardier was shot in the elbow, causing serious injury. The beer had to be salvoed to get to him. That was the end of the egg runs.

For security reasons, no personal written records were permitted of these missions; therefore, after 45 years, memories become dull, but some of the targets we attacked were Lashio, Myitkyina, and warehouses, railroads, bridges and airports along the Burma Road from Mandalay in the south to Paoshan in the north.

During November or early December, 1944, five or six crews were sent on detached service to establish a tent city at Yunnanyi, to reduce the travel time to targets. As I had served in the infantry for two years prior to transferring to the Air Corps, it appeared I knew how to properly raise a six-man squad tent. Thereafter, our crew had to assist everyone in setting up their tents. I tried to tell them the tent pegs and poles had to be in alignment but they did not believe me until the C.O. arrived. Then they believed!

While at Yunnanyi, there were the usual "house boys" who were always around. One day it was noticed that one of them made a visit to the bulletin board when the flight schedules were posted. Shortly thereafter, he would slowly saunter away from camp across the rice paddies. Finally, it was decided he could read English and was passing the flight information to the enemy. After watching him, the MP's gave chase. Upon being challenged, he ran instead of halting, so they shot him. This episode taught us to be more careful as to who was allowed to read the bulletin board.

Merrill's Marauders were moving southward, clearing out the Japanese in the heavy jungle south of Myitkyina. We were sent there for a short while, on detached service. The first planes that landed there were fired on by straggling enemy troops, before all of them left or were captured.

After returning to Yangkai in December, 1944, we went to Nanning, which was a temporary staging base for a planned attack on Japanese navy ships that had moved into the South China Sea. No sooner had we arrived there than the weather socked in so badly the attack was canceled. The weather did not deter the Japanese from bombing us that night, however.

Sometime during December, the 11th and 22nd Bomb Squadrons joined in an attack on a harbor on Hainan Island in the South China Sea. There were also many fighter-escorted B-24s on this mission. We successfully damaged shipping, warehouses, wharves and the airfield. Many of our planes received damage, some serious, but all those in the 22nd's flight returned safely.

Of the few high altitude attacks we flew, one was particularly dangerous for me. As I recall, the target was a bridge in Indochina. During the bomb run, I had to leave the tail gunner's position to take the bomb damage assessment photographs with a K-17 camera, through the aft photo hatch. As many of us will recall, this camera is large, quite heavy and difficult to handle, but it did take excellent pictures. Upon completion of the bomb run, I returned to the tail position only to see that a large 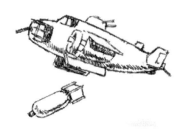 caliber shell had passed through the seat and canopy. Had I not been taking those pictures, that shell would have gone through me from bottom to top. There must have been someone flying with us that day who was not on the flight roster.

On January 10th, 1945, our crew was grounded after successfully completing fifty-one combat missions. My records show I had logged 192.20 hours of combat flying.

In February, 1945, thirty-one men from Yangkai were rotated to the States, having completed their tour of duty in China. Originally, my name was on this list but was removed as I had inadequate time in the theater.

When the C-46 in which they were traveling left Chabua, it went off course and hit a mountain peak near Tibet. There was only one survivor, S/Sgt. Marvin H. Jacobs, a radio gunner from the 22nd Bomb Squadron, who was rescued in a very dangerous and dramatic effort by the medical corps; a sad ending for men who had served faithfully, under difficult conditions, for so long.

Lt. John Stevens, our navigator-bombardier, was rotated to the United States in December, 1944. I, the flight engineer-gunner, was rotated in April, 1945, and Dominic Villanti, gunner, and Louis Dorn, radio operator, in May, 1945. Major Francis Fensel, our pilot and squadron operations officer, remained with the 22nd Bomb Squadron until the war ended. I understand he logged over one hundred combat missions.

John A. Johns
MEMORIES OF CHAKULIA

FAMILY PUMPING ALL DAY
AND NIGHT LONG

In the middle of our camp in Chakulia was an old-fashioned, iron water pump that needed constant hand pumping. There was an Indian hired to keep our huge water tank filled, high above the shower stall. To keep up the flow of that tremendous amount of water, that poor soul had to pump constantly, 24 hours a day! To accomplish this, he enlisted the aid of his family. We paid this man 14 cents a day!! That was for the whole family.

The British bristled when they heard of the salary. They strongly felt that amount was horrendously inflated! By the way, I don't think that pump was ever oiled. We heard that squeaking all night long.

BRITISH AND AMERICAN JUSTICE

I was sent from Chakulia to Jamshedpur to represent a couple of our enlisted men that had an accident with a British vehicle on a sharp turn of the road between Chakulia and Jamshedpur.

At the British compound we met in a tent for lunch (kidneys). Great! It was at lunch that we determined that it wasn't necessary to hold a formal court. It was suggested by the gentlemanly host that we certainly would be in agreement that the accident came about because we both drove on the wrong side of the road. Agreement was unanimous.

AS OFFICER OF THE DAY

We had just been robbed, early that day. I became officer of the day that night. The first duty I had was to follow up on a lead that there was a native that had a stash of money. I entered his home and went into a room that was piled high with wheat. Underneath that pile, I was told, was all the money. The native shoveled all that wheat into another room. Once the wheat was removed, there in the middle of the dirt floor was a buried metal can with a slot in the top. The can was dug up and opened to reveal about a dozen rupees. Value: three dollars!

GRAINS OF RICE

I was given a few days leave and boarded the train in Chakulia on its way to Calcutta, about 80 miles to the east. There was no room in the passenger sections. It was offered that I ride in one of the freight cars. Looking forward to visiting the great city of Calcutta, it was accepted that I sit amongst the piled-up sacks and boxes awaiting delivery. Very slowly, we rolled on our way east.

At our first stop, the train was packed, mostly with children. The car I was in had a wooden floor with slats widely spaced. Looking through those slats, I noticed many excited children under the car. They hadn't even waited for the train to stop—they rushed to get under the car, but for what?

I came out of my car, anxious to find what was going on. Bending down to get a closer look, I saw the children were pushing, dusting around in the dirt, and picking up grains of rice that had fallen through the slats of the floor of the freight car! This scene occurred each time we jerked to a stop at a village on our way to Calcutta.

Eventually we arrived. Even though I was looking forward to spending leave in one of the largest cities in India, the strong image evoked in that train ride took the edge off the visitation.

MORE ABOUT
THE CHIANG MAI RAID

I remember that we were really going to stretch the distance the fully loaded B-25 travels. If you note the time over the target (1815) and the time of landing (2215)—that's <u>half</u> the trip! What we accomplished was an <u>impossible</u> flight of eight hours!! The "normal" maximum trip for a fully loaded B-25 is from six to six and one half hours!

What we all did, once in the air, was to pull back on the gas and air mixture to where the engines were almost running rough and hot—it worked. We flew at high altitude until we were 20 to 30 miles from our target—then spiraled down to about 200 feet, and then proceeded on to the target. About seven to ten miles north of the airfield we flew over a number of barracks. There were a few soldiers scurrying about looking up at us. At this time we were really flying low, 50 to 100 feet off the ground. When we arrived at the airfield they were ready for us. Their gunners were firing from both sides of the field, creating an umbrella of bullets that we had to fly through. Even though the gunners were ready for us, the other personnel and pilots were not. Their planes were still parked and tied down on both sides of their runway.

The reason for the mission was that we had been notified by our spies that the Japs were readying an air raid on Kunming. Excitedly, we made pass after pass, strafing, dropping bombs and dropping them ridiculously low, but we did destroy a number of their bombers. They did not run a bombing mission on Kunming.

Yes, we were peppered, running through that umbrella of fire. We regrouped, all of us, and headed home. We did encounter much cloud cover that we welcomed, to protect us from enemy fire or planes. But our trip was constantly in and out of clouds. We lost each other frequently and returned single file.

The plane I was on crash landed; we hadn't realized how badly we were hit until we attempted to land. Our hydraulic lines were cut so that we couldn't lower our landing gear. We all walked away from that landing.

PAINTING THE
SHERIDAN EXPRESS

The story of Ann Sheridan's visit to Yangkai by Jim White, later in this book, prompted me to write. You see, I am the artist that Jim alludes to who painted the "Sheridan Express" on one of our planes, for that visit.

It was flattering when the request came through that I do something. Shortly after I said I would, we discovered no artist brushes nor paint. We also knew it had to be accomplished that morning for their visit that afternoon!

House paint was found, and for a brush I frayed a rough rope and tied about two inches of it on a stick. Armed with a "quick" sketch, the paint and my brush, I was on a scaffold and painted the "Sheridan Express" that morning, what was left of it. I had no photo of Ann Sheridan but I knew she was a sexy red head and my paint job emphasized that hair.

The paint was still wet when our guests arrived, and as the Jeep passed by where I and many, many others were standing, straining to get a good look— there she was, in all her glory—an unkempt dishwater blonde!

PICKED UP NEW B-25
WITH CANNON

I was sent down to Calcutta from our base in China to pick up a new B-25. When some of the newly arrived men heard of my assignment I was asked to hunt for and pick up their foot lockers that had not yet been delivered. It took some doing. The foot lockers were finally found in a huge warehouse in Dum Dum. To accommodate about six foot lockers, I had to make a shelf with some two by fours in the bomb bay of the new plane.

So, over the Hump again. We stopped at Kunming, then continued north to Yangkai. The men who were most anxious to get their lockers knew of my landing time. I was warmly greeted by the men, until I opened the bomb bay doors! There was much liquid dripping from the plane. I thought it was gasoline, but to the horror of the men the foot lockers were opened. The contents were soaked.

Pans, buckets, etc., were desperately found and there was much wringing of clothing trying to save what was left of the whiskey. Bottles were busted or uncorked while flying high over the Hump. I was not a very popular fellow for quite a while.

A LITTLE EXCHANGE

One of the pluses of our move over the Hump was to make money by exchanging rupees for dollars! The exchange was something like four or six to one! The value of Chinese money was almost nil. Owners of businesses actually took their money to banks in piled-high wheel barrows. Thus the rupee was highly regarded.

When you had an assignment to make a round trip over the Hump, many of the men would give you rupees to exchange for them. All you had to do was stand at any corner in Kunming and the money exchanger would find you. Once they heard of the amount of rupees I had, they told me they couldn't handle that much on the street. I was told to follow the contact man.

We went into the deep, deep bowels of Kunming, through homes, courtyards and finally arrived at our destination. I ended up in a bedroom of a house and was told to wait. The room was just large enough to hold a bed, with barely enough space to walk around that bed. All the while that I waited, I had my hand on my trusty Colt 45. Finally, two dapper gentlemen appeared. They wore derby hats, camel hair coats and spats— highly polished shoes. One of them pulled out a huge wad of dollars and 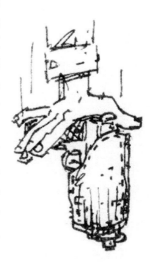 peeled off the necessary amount for the exchange. I was told to follow the contact person back to where he found me. All the while back, I was fearful of being robbed and killed.

David K. Hayward
THAT FIRST MISSION

It was my first mission, April 8, 1943, and I soon thought it was to be my last.

Our formation consisted of ten planes. We had no fighter escort. I was flying as copilot, as it was the practice to put newly-arrived pilots in the copilot's seat for seasoning. Lt. Loyal G. "LG" Brown was the pilot and had been "seasoned" already, after about 40 combat missions.

We arrived at the Meiktila airdrome, a Japanese airfield near Mandalay, Burma. After dropping our bombs on the field, we turned to head for home.

Normally that was a happy time, the first real feeling of relief for the day. Even the sandwiches that were provided for us tasted good, although we always wondered whether those black specks in the bread were bugs of some kind. Indeed, often they were.

I looked out and down through my copilot's window and saw, to my great alarm, a formation of Japanese airplanes below us, heading in the same direction as we were. I counted twenty one of them. There might have been more.

I picked up the radio mike and tried to spread the word, but by that time a lot of other people were trying to do the same thing, none very effectively.

Every minute or two (probably every few seconds) I looked down. I soon recognized that the Japanese formation was comprised of both fighters and bombers and even worse, they were gaining altitude on us fast and would soon be alongside of us.

LG Brown and I were flying "Old Number 13," the oldest and slowest plane in the 22nd Bomb Squadron; certainly, it was

227

the slowest plane that day and we were flying as "tail end Charlie." (I learned later that Old 13 had been bellied in by Wil McDowell some months earlier and had been patched up to fly again.)

The pilot of the lead plane must have pushed his throttles forward to the firewall, because all the planes except ours took off for home base, leaving us behind.

Due to the meaningless screaming and confusion on the radio, the lead ship was apparently unaware that Old 13 was being left behind without the protective shield of all the guns that could be brought to bear from the other planes in the formation. A lone bomber amidst a swarm of Zeros does not have much of a chance of survival.

Before long, our turret gunner called on the intercom to report that a Jap Zero was doing a slow roll in the blind spot of our tail.

A little while later I looked out of my window and could see right into the cockpit of a Zero. I'll tell you, I did some praying and philosophizing about that time.

I had seen movies about the predicaments of flying and, as far as I could remember, none of the great ones such as James Cagney or Pat O'Brien had ever faced anything like this.

Well, as far as I know, there was not a shot fired. The Japs went away. Why? I don't know exactly. Perhaps "Someone" up there was looking out for us. Perhaps the Jap pilot thought we weren't worth the trouble, or he was just trying to show off. Perhaps the Japs had something else on their minds. It could have been all of the above.

My guess is that the formation of Japanese planes had taken off just before our arrival, on its way to bomb a target in India and we stumbled upon them accidentally. If so, it is likely that their fighters had been instructed to avoid possible decoys and to fight only if their own bombers were attacked.

Perhaps the Jap pilots had seen American movies, showing how clever James Cagney and Pat O'Brien were and had suspected that those "crafty Americans" were playing a trick on them. Who knows?

When we finally returned to home base at Chakulia, I kissed the ground.

Were all the rest of the missions going to be this bad? If so, how could I possibly make it through? LG Brown tried to be consoling, saying that this mission wasn't so bad, considering some he had been on.

In the weeks to come, around the club at night, we heard similar stories about a lone Zero that would approach our planes, perform slow rolls in the blind spot of the tail section of the B-25, scare the daylights out of the crew and then leave without firing a shot.

Finally, we heard, the Zero tried it once too often. An American fighter pilot caught him in the act and put a stop to it for once and for all.

A BOONDOGGLE OVER TIBET

In April of 1943, very soon after arriving in India, I was flying as copilot with Patrick L. Ham who had been stationed in Assam province, in the northeastern part of India, prior to coming into the 22nd Bomb Squadron and who was familiar with flying in that part of India. Our commanding officer asked Pat if his crew would volunteer to go on a series of single-plane B-25 raids into northern Burma from Dinjan, an airfield in Assam.

This seemed to be a welcome change from Chakulia, so we agreed to go. During the four combat missions that we made into northern Burma, we found our targets, made our bomb runs and returned safely to Dinjan. These were the only missions of mine in which we had fighter escort.

During off hours at Dinjan, life was pleasant. We stayed in a tea planter's bungalow, one of those places on stilts, with screening all four sides. Native bearers served every need. The food was good by India standards.

In those days while living on the tea plantation, I felt as though I was being projected into one of the novels by Somerset Maugham, a favorite author of mine at the time. The British influence was very much in evidence.

Our bombardier/navigator was one of several Tokyo raiders that had been assigned to our squadron. In the evenings as we walked along a country road, he told stories of that famous mission. He explained that he and his fellow raiders had been in India for a year since the raid and were anxious to go home or be assigned to a different theater of the war. For him, to be shot down and captured by the Japanese would likely result in execution, as had happened to some of those who were captured after the Tokyo raid.

Then came something unexpected. On the next day at the airfield, a colonel walked up to Pat Ham and wanted to borrow our B-25 and fly into the Himalayas to look for a Japanese radio homing station that had been luring our transport planes off course.

He needed our twin engine plane and its radio compass. Pat didn't care about going along, nor did our navigator, but I was eager and offered to go as the colonel's copilot on this new adventure.

Soon after takeoff I began to wonder if this was just a boondoggle. But in the military, one is reluctant to "reason why." It was generally known that the Air Transport Command had reported false homing signals, which they thought had been generated by the Japanese in order to pull our planes off course and into a fiery crash in the mountains.

Once in flight we followed the Brahmaputra River valley northwesterly into Tibet, not at all in an easterly direction where our transport planes would likely be flying. Tibet was a neutral country. We had been told not to go there for fear of being interned for the duration of the war, if forced down.

The skies were clear and the view was breathtaking. I saw a glaciated valley that was much larger than the Yosemite Valley in California that I knew so well. Primitive people were living along the steep sides of the U-shaped valley. I thought of my junior college geology class. Hanging tributaries fed water into the meandering river in the valley floor far below.

In the distance, we saw mountain ranges on both sides of us and at about the same altitude that we were flying, 20,000 feet. I took photos of the rugged mountains as we flew by.

Even with our superchargers on, the B-25 wouldn't climb much higher without stalling the plane. Finally, the valley narrowed and turned sharply toward the north. At our last chance to do so, the colonel made a 180 degree turn, being careful not to bank too steeply and stall out at this altitude. We headed back the same way that we came, landing at Dinjan after what my flight log recorded as a two and one-half hour flight.

Ten people had been aboard; most of whom I think were just along for the scenic ride. Ordinarily, the B-25 is a five-man plane. That night I heard our passengers complaining about the splitting headaches they had. Was it any wonder? Only five oxygen outlets were available on the plane. The pilot and I had our own outlets. The other eight people had to share the remaining three oxygen masks while cruising at about 20,000 feet altitude for most of those two and one-half hours.

We had flown into Tibet without a map of the area. I don't know how close we flew to the capital city of Llasa, but by dead reckoning I think we covered about half the distance and we certainly saw some spectacular scenery en route.

I would like to have shown the folks back home some photographs of the Potala on the hill overlooking Llasa. But half a loaf is better than none and a boondoggle such as this was not likely to happen again.

And, oh yes! We never did find or even look for the reported Japanese homing station!

James M. White
IT MUST HAVE BEEN
SOMETHING I ATE

It was early March, '44, about 2:00 p.m. when we touched down at the Bengal Air Depot in Bangalore, India, having completed about 55 hours of flying time since leaving Georgia. The flight had been unusual from two aspects. To begin with, we were told that ours was the first B-25J to be deployed overseas. We had trained on the G and H models. The J would be modified while at Bangalore and we would proceed to Yangkai and the 22nd Bomb Squadron via Air Transport Command (ATC).

Beyond that, the entire trip had been flown solo—at no time were we in the presence of other aircraft, this despite the fact that all crews having a dead reckoning (DR) navigator only were to be accompanied by an ATC celestial navigator. We did not know this at the time. I was a simple-minded bombardier/DR navigator.

The trip, with interim stops in Puerto Rico, Trinidad, Guiana, Belem and Natal, Brazil, Ascension Island, plus Kano, Maiduguri and Khartoum in Africa, Aden, Masira Island and Karachi, had been fairly mundane. Quite obviously, compensating errors in my navigation made it possible for us to hit each interim stop as scheduled. During the trip, Lee Baker had been very generous, allowing me to take over the controls for about half of the time. The crew included Lt. Lee Baker (pilot), S/Sgt. Les Sejarto (radio man), Sgt. Joe Christofinelli (engineer) and Sgt. Al Carroll (tail gunner). We also carried an additional gunner as a passenger. Baker and I were 22 years old while the others ranged to Al Carroll's 18 years.

On the ground, at Bangalore, we were ravenous. Breakfast in Karachi had been many hours earlier. Much to our dismay, we found the mess hall closed. Undaunted by this fact, I approached

the mess sergeant and informed him that the crew had to be fed. He stubbornly refused, telling me that the mess hall would reopen at 5 p.m. I persisted, telling him that army regs dictated our enlisted crew members be fed three times daily. He finally relented and at the same time, told me that Lee and I could also eat as it wasn't that much trouble to handle two more. We had what I thought was a damned good lunch.

The following morning, I knew that something was amiss—my worst expectations—I had a beautiful case of "whistling trots" while all the others felt great. We were scheduled to leave Bangalore for Calcutta on an ATC Gooney Bird. The C-47 had been sitting in the hot Indian sun for several hours before we emplaned.

Cabin temperature was well in excess of 100 degrees. Typical of ATC aircraft, the bird was equipped with a single portable chemical "John" which I occupied for the entire trip. On arrival at Calcutta, I was too weak to get off the aircraft by myself. Baker and the crew helped me off and took me to the base dispensary where my temperature was found to be something in excess of 105 degrees. Because of a major smallpox outbreak filling the hospital in Calcutta, I was put in a tent at the Dum Dum orphanage. As virtually the only inhabitant of this "Tent City," mine was next to the tent that was set up as a latrine.

For the first twelve hours, I sat on one stool while upchucking in the next, thinking I was going to die and worried I might not. After five days at the orphanage before being released for further travel, I caught up with my crew in Chabua. Often in the years which followed this experience, I have thought, "Did that mess sergeant slip me a mickey of some sort because I was so obnoxious about feeding our crew?" Nah—he wouldn't do anything like that—or would he?

LATRINE LULUS

Never let it be said that the 22nd Bomb Squadron latrine at Yangkai was dull and prosaic. As the following vignettes suggest, it could be a veritable booby trap fraught with danger:

AN ELECTRIFYING EXPERIENCE

One of the more diabolically clever officers (name withheld) was also somewhat of an electrical genius—a talent he had honed while a cadet at Hudson High (U.S. Military Academy). In his travels, he had acquired an extremely lifelike fly fabricated of copper or some equally conductive material. Using very fine wire, he connected the fly to a high capacity storage battery which was then hidden outside the latrine. He next placed the fly on the upper slope of the trough type urinal, a distance of some several feet from the drain at the lower end of the trough. The sinister scene was now set. In due course, a totally unsuspecting fly boy dropped in to dispose of that second or third cup of coffee

239

he had consumed during breakfast. Spotting the fly and having the mentality of the typical throttle jockey, this stalwart decided he would steer it toward the drain by directing his stream at the fly—ZAP!

BOTTOM ROUND ROAST

One of the duties of the Squadron CQ (in Charge of Quarters) was that of pouring a liberal amount of aviation gas through the openings in our multi-holer and then igniting it about an hour before arrival of the "honey bucket" brigade. I do not know the rationale behind this ritual but can swear that it was performed. This little exercise was usually done at about 0400 hours—not a particularly busy time of the day at Ye Olde Latrine. On this occasion, the CQ, after pouring the gas, realized that he had no matches. Cursing beneath his breath, he set out in search of igniters. Within a minute or so, probably as the result of imbibing in too much Jing Bao juice, one of our laddies visited the John to sit and ponder life's imponderables. Lighting up a cigarette, he tossed the still flaming match into the adjoining hole—POW! How do you like yours done: rare, medium rare or well done?

WHATEVER HAPPENED TO
OLD WHAT'S HIS NAME?

Over the years, I have scanned each new membership directory looking, often in vain, for a particular friend or acquaintance from my days with the 22nd Bomb Squadron. Why is it so many are not there? This seems especially true of some of the real characters of that time. Often times while reading the Jing Bao Journal, I will think—whatever happened to old:

WHISPERING RAY BOHANNON. So called because it was said of Ray that he was the only man in the 14th Air Force who could call the tower from 5,000 feet without using the radio.

Perpetual custodian of the squadron drinking hat, Ray had started his pilot days as a sergeant. When I first met Ray, he was a flight officer up for promotion to second lieutenant. The board,

 headed by Col. Wells, group C.O., had convened in the mess hall at Yangkai. Just as the board was exiting the hearing, Ray was asked by a friend as to what he thought his chances might be. In a voice that was probably heard in Kunming, Ray responded, "How the hell should I know? As far as I'm concerned old Preacher Wells can shove that gold bar up his ... sideways." Ray was promoted.

MAJOR EDISON WEATHERLY, squadron CO at the time of my assignment to the 22nd, a real "Fearless Fosdick" in the truest sense of the word. The sort who would charge in like a raging bull in situations where angels fear to tread. During his extended

241

tour he probably collected more holes in his airplane than one would find in 5 pounds of Swiss cheese.

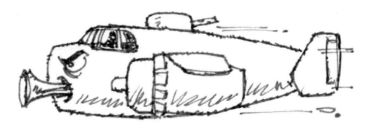

His great unrealized dream was to meet up with a Kawanishi flying boat that he would down with one well directed blast from his 75 mm cannon. Fascinated by the 75, he also dreamed of encountering an elephant on one of the trails in French Indochina—what a hell of an elephant gun that would be.

THE REVEREND JESSE E. FOWLER.
Actually Second Lieutenant Jesse E. Fowler, a bombardier from Yazoo City, Mississippi. Resembling nothing more than an impish leprechaun, Jesse claimed to be an ordained minister. As he told it, he had done every mean, lowdown thing in the book—boozed it up, chased broads, had a few run-ins with John Law and a half dozen other similar deeds.  Seems he was sitting in an outhouse one day when suddenly he saw the light and was born again. Jesse, being a newcomer to the squadron, had drawn an upper bunk. The sounds rolling out of his bunk while he was reading were hilarious—"Well, I swan"—"Declare"—"Whooee." The only problem was we had no idea as to what he was reading, as he alternated between the Bible and Punsi's porn. When not reading he would stand for hours

throwing his jungle knife at a tree—"Never know when I might have to throw at a Japanese."

MAJOR BILL SURGINER. Bill, a concert violinist, was a late comer to the squadron, having flown a little L-5 liaison plane in Burma before joining the 22nd. It must have been great fun for a major to transition from an L-5 to a B-25 and wind up flying copilot for a 1st or 2nd lieutenant. This never seemed to bother him in the least. He was an extremely quiet and reserved sort, somewhat of an introvert, or so it seemed. One day while Bill was in his upper bunk, "Cowboy" Earl Elder ambled in with his guitar. Earl must know a thousand or more country-western songs. He had scarcely begun one when we heard a whoop and a holler from Bill's bunk. Leaping to the floor, he grabbed for his violin which suddenly became a fiddle. It seems like that concert violinist's second love was fiddling—no introvert here.

CAPT. HOWARD "GOODIE" GOODELL. Goodie joined the squadron as a captain. I had first met him in Columbia, SC, where he was assigned as an instructor pilot. Now, some six months after my arrival, he was suddenly a squadron mate. A West Point graduate, this was the original laid-back guy. Nothing seemed to bother him, including paying attention to what he was doing at the moment. One day I lucked out and wound up flying with him as his navigator. We were flying right wing in a three plane sortie. Returning from the target, we were in an area where a flight of Japanese fighters had been reported within the last hour. As is usually the case, the "pucker" factor increased by some moderate degree. The flight leader directed the formation to tighten up—a reasonable sort of request given the circumstances.

Within a minute, the left wing ship was as close to the lead ship as a flea is to the monkey's back. Not old Goodie—we were at least a mile wide of the others and about a mile behind. I suggested that we might want to get a little closer but Goodie was having none of that. We just continued to loaf along, never drawing closer than a mile to the others. Fortunately, the Japanese fighter threat never materialized and we arrived home unscathed. Equally as fortunate, I never again was to fly with Goodie.

CAPT. ROBERT McCARTHY. Old Bob McCarthy must have been in training for the demolition derby. Fly with him once and there could be no doubt as to the veracity of that statement. Fly with him a second time only after conferring with your friendly insurance agent and making appropriate arrangements with "Digger O'Dell," the neighborhood mortician. On one occasion when I was fortunate enough to ride with "Crash" McCarthy, we were pulling close to the lead ship; left wing down, we were approaching from the right. When Bob felt we were close enough, he brought the left wing up only to find that we were four feet inside the wing tip of number one. The resultant bang as the wings collided turned my Jockeys to a soft brown color. On still another occasion, we were returning to Yangkai from Yunnanyi and I was positioned in the navigator's compartment. On our final approach, we came in a little high. For the first time in my career in B-25s I was able to view the runway—through the glass hatch above Bob's head.

W.O. POWELL. First Lieutenant W.O. Powell, a soft-talking, easy going Texan, was a delight to be around. Totally unassuming, he could amuse you with some of the most outrageous Texas tales one can imagine. During June of '44, some of us from the 22nd had been sent on TDY (temporary duty) to Malir Air Base, just outside Karachi. The reason given was that we were to train in the use of the 75 mm cannon. Why me, was a mystery as I had about six months training in the H model before being assigned to the 22nd. At any rate, I wound up sharing a room with "W.O." and "whispering" Ray Bohannon. It was a particularly hot afternoon and the three of us were lying on our canvas cots and swilling beer and swapping war stories. Ray was fiddling with his Colt 45. Apparently, the beer had gotten to W.O. as he announced that he was making a trip to the head. Deciding to take a short cut, he exited through the rear window of the room. Just as he cleared the sill, Ray triggered off a shot at one of the blades in the slow moving punkah overhead. The sound was deafening. W.O. dropped from sight. Moments later we saw his hands on the window sill, knuckles white, then slowly his face appeared—as white as the knuckles. "What the hell was that?" he asked in a quivering voice. When assured that Ray had

not fired at him, he went on his way. At this point, Ray, taking very deliberate aim, emptied the clip. Not one blade was touched. Then from the door we heard, "Are you finished, Ray?" Standing in the doorway was Lt. Col. "Wee Willy" Willis, resplendent in a tailor-made, lime-green safari-type uniform. When assured that Ray was indeed finished. "Wee Willy" told Ray that he wanted to see him on the roof the next afternoon, replacing the red tile shingles he had blown away.

LET ME SHOW YOU
HOW IT'S DONE

Yangkai—summer of '44. The 22nd Bomb Squadron is blessed with an abundance of copilots. These poor hapless creatures were no doubt the result of stateside training conducted in the dual-control B-25J.

By now, production of the mighty H model with its single pilot's station had come to end the need for so many copilots.

Production teams at North American's plant in Kansas City were grinding out J's by the thousands (more than 4,300 would be produced by war's end).

Unfortunately for the copilots, because of aircraft pipeline problems, the 22nd Bomb Squadron inventory of aircraft was heavy on H's, with but a handful of the J model. This meant the typical copilot might be required to spend ten years in the 14th Air Force to complete 50 missions. Taking pity on these poor souls, the Squadron initiated a training program in which they would be upgraded to first pilot.

On this particular day, one of our more senior pilots, a seasoned combat captain with many hundreds of hours of B-25 left seat time, was guiding a copilot through landing procedures.

Positioned in the right hand seat of one of the few dual control models, he was the consummate teacher.

"Let's bank a little more to the left—we have a pretty fair cross wind," he said as they turned on final approach. Then, "Great, we're right in the slot but still a little too hot—back off a bit. Steady—steady—nice and easy—let's make this one a grease job." A few hundred feet of descent and then, "Okay, back off a bit and start our flare out." Nearing touchdown, he enthused, "Fantastic! Chop throttles and back on the controls—oooh no— we forgot to lower the landing gear."

Scratch one Baker Two Five!

ROGER B-25, GIVE ME A CALL ON YOUR DOWNWIND

Sometimes as I lie on my bunk, having nothing better to do when we are not flying, I reflect upon those days when we were training at Columbia, South Carolina. It was the fall of '43, Myrtle Beach, S.C. It is a miserably cold and cloudy day. Several B-25s out of Columbia are engaged in gunnery practice. Leo Baker's crew consisting of Baker, Sgts. Les Sejarto, Joe Christofanelli and Allison Carroll, along with yours truly is assigned to low level, 75 mm firing against targets anchored in heavily rolling seas. On this day, we are flying in an older "G" model. We are destined to be assigned to China and the 22nd Bomb Squadron within several months. An instructor pilot occupies the right seat.

Moments earlier, one of the earlier model B-25s had inadvertently sprayed several rounds of .50 caliber into the Ocean Forest Hotel on the beach, no doubt spicing up the lives of its inhabitants. Seems the guy manning the bottom turret became disoriented by 180 degrees and let fly inland rather than out to sea (the bottom turret would soon be removed from all B-25s).

Lee is now lining up for our third pass, having scored direct hits on two earlier runs. He makes his initial sighting as I prepare to load the cannon. Placing the shell on the loading tray, I push it forward only to have it hang up with the projectile in the barrel and most of the shell case still resting on the loading tray. We were later to learn that the loading tray was askew by several degrees, causing the shell to enter the tube while canted to the left. At this point, assuring me of his expertise with the cannon, Joe Christofanelli attempts to drive the shell home using the wooden ramrod. Foiled in this attempt, he now faces the rear and attempts to kick the shell in using the heel of his G.I. boots—no joy. With a triumphant gleam in his eyes he seizes an empty shell case and hooks the rear rim of the empty shell over the rim of the lodged shell and gives a mighty yank. Swoosh—out comes the lodged shell casing, but without the projectile. In the process, several pounds of black powder are spilled on the loading tray.

Having turned to caution both pilots against smoking, I look back just in time to see Joe place a new shell on the tray and shove it forward. There is a soft explosion and flames shoot back from the lodged projectile to the large mound of black powder causing immediate ignition. Within seconds, the entire navigator's section is afire with flames reaching the astrodome.

Joe, in panic, has me pinned tightly against the navigation table. Yelling for him to get the front fire extinguisher, I push him forward and launch myself over the bomb bay to secure the rear extinguisher.

Shoving my head into the radio compartment, I scream for the extinguisher. Les Sejarto, a scant two feet from my head, asks, "What did you say?" Al Carroll, a full twenty feet away, is on his feet in a flash—grabbing the extinguisher. He flings it in my direction. Within seconds, I am emerging once again into the navigation compartment, spewing foam at the flames. Joe is spraying foam from a position immediately behind the pilots.

By now, convinced of an immediate explosion, Lee Baker chops the throttles and prepares to ditch the aircraft. As our extinguishers empty, we see the fire is now almost under control. Using our feet to stamp out the embers, we attempt to stifle what fire remains.

Seeing our progress, Lee now slams the throttles forward and pulls back on the wheel. Shuddering and shaking like a Blue Tick Hound passing an oversize bone, our valiant lady makes a stab at recovery. For what seems an eternity, we stagger forward, flirting dangerously with a full stall.

Finally, gaining control, Lee turns and starts a straight approach to the Myrtle Beach airstrip calling, "MAYDAY, MAYDAY," as we near the field.

Out of the ether, a rather laconic voice says, "Roger, B-25, give me a call when you are on your downwind."

"Downwind, my butt," Baker barks, "I'm on fire and on my final now."

A moment's pause and then, "But you can't land now, I have a P-39 landing now and the pilot has no radio contact."

"To hell with your P-39, he can cover his own tail," spits out Baker. We see the P-39 touch down and slow almost immediately. We are now just several hundred feet from touchdown. Suddenly the fighter jock looks back and spots us about to cream him. A quick movie double-take on his part and he slams his throttle forward, making for the wild blue like a homesick angel, as we slap down. Another second or two and we would have been chewing on his butt with our props.

Rolling to a stop, Lee pulls off on a taxi strip and cuts the engines. Within seconds, all six are out of the plane and on a dead run for safer ground. Pulling up after a hundred yards or so, we sit down and without a word, pull out the old butts and fire up—each deep in his own thoughts. Finally, "Hey, White, how in hell did you go over the bomb bay head first and then come back out in the navigator's compartment head first without getting

off the bomb bay?" With me at six one and 190 pounds and with clear access over the bomb bay restricted to about two feet in width by about 18 inches in height at most, it seems like a damn good question.

Joe is missing his left eyebrow and I my right. Much of the hair on the side and top of my head is frizzled like a matron's bad perm. My chest harness has one strap burned completely through and my B-4 flight jacket is missing most of the sheepskin collar. Al Carroll tells of turning around and spotting, then tackling, Les Sejarto who is about to bail out with the airplane now at about 100 feet.

After about ten minutes we venture back into the airplane. We see the underside of the navigator's table is badly charred and the plastic knobs, which control release of the 75 mm shells, have melted. The rack is still holding 18 unused shells. The astrodome will never again accommodate a sextant. We were to learn later that a bomb bay auxiliary gas tank had been installed in this airplane until two days back. The fuel lines supporting this tank had run through the navigator's compartment until the tank was removed.

"Roger, B-25, give me a call on your downwind."

LET'S HAVE A LITTLE DECORUM
IF YOU PLEASE

While a member of the 22nd Bomb Squadron, I served under three squadron C.O.'s, Major Edison Weatherly, Major Loren Nickels, and Lt. Colonel Philip Main. I will not date this tale, as it would allow the reader to determine which of the three was C.O. at the time of the action described therein.

The atmosphere was somewhat quiet and subdued around Yangkai, as we had been under the influence of inclement weather for several days on end—boring to say the least. Someone suggested a poker game. Sounded like fun and I quickly joined in, as my poker luck had been a little short of fantastic of late. I had won enough during the past month that I was able to send several hundred bucks back home to my mother so she could buy the diamond engagement ring I had never given to my beautiful bride Evelyn.

We started out with but four players, not much fun but better than a poke in the eye with a sharp stick. In any event, several of the enlisted personnel, including Al Carroll, tail gunner for our crew, were watching and kibitzing. I had never been much on the difference between a commissioned officer and a non-com. What the hell, these guys flew with us and would die with us if we got hit, why shouldn't they be able to play a friendly game of cards with us? I finally asked if they would care to jump in. There was no need to ask a second time. We were now six in number.

We had been playing about ten or fifteen minutes when I was dealt a dream hand. The game was jacks or better. On the initial deal, I had a pair of tens and some garbage. I discarded the cruddy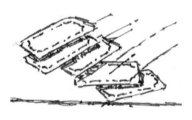

253

cards and asked for three new ones. Imagine my surprise to find another pair of tens in the three I was dealt. Here I sit with four tens and nothing wild in the game. I figure that I am looking down everyone's throat. Not wanting to scare off any of those I would be scalping, I opened with a very modest bet.

I figured all five would stay with me. Four of the others folded without even asking for new cards.

The fifth guy asked for one card, obviously trying to fill to an inside straight or to catch a flush. He didn't get his card and threw in without further challenge to me. I had to settle for the ante and the buck or two opening bet as my winnings on that hand.

A short time later, I was dealt aces full. Again, as before, I made a very modest opening bet hoping that all would participate in the hand. Several saw my opening bet and asked for cards. After viewing their new cards, two dropped out leaving one other player against me. I made what I thought was a very modest second bet hoping he had made a hand and would raise me.

He simply called. Once again, I had made very little on a terrific hand.

Suddenly, my luck shifted to the opposite side of the table and into the hands of Al Carroll. After several games of five and seven card stud it was back again to jacks or better and once again I couldn't believe my luck. This time I had kings full. Al saw me and raised—hot damn, I had fresh meat. I immediately bumped him back. He smiled rather smugly and raised me one more time. We had now raised three times and could raise no more. With a wicked grin on my face, I slapped down my full boat and started to reach for the pot. "Not so fast, lieutenant," said Al as he put his four ladies on the table.

About twenty minutes later, I was dealt four aces—I had a lock on this one. I had never seen so many outstanding poker hands in a single game as we saw that night. Again, Al Carroll stayed with me, raising me on my opening bet. I had him this time and was going to make him pay for that last one. I raised

him big time—let him grin that New Hampshire ploy boy smile this time! He banged me right back with a raise as big as mine had been—man this is going to be great. You could have heard a pin drop when he laid down his cards—a very pretty queen high straight flush. I damn near dirtied my drawers. Al had cleaned me out that night.

To add injury to insult, the old man summoned me to his room the next day and reamed my butt out for having fraternized with the enlisted men.

ONE DOWN,
FORTY-NINE TO GO

It was April 8, 1944. We had taken off at 1:45 am and, with the moon sliding behind a cloud cover, it was dark as hell. Moments earlier, we had overflown Lao Kay, which meant we were now over French Indochina and well into enemy territory. We were en route to Hainan Island for a pre-dawn, low-level, para-frag attack on the Jap fighter strip. Our mission was to be a fighter-suppression prelude to a high level bombing strike by B-24s, who would be targeting several Japanese heavy cruisers refueling.

Two elements of two planes each from the 22nd Squadron were to fly to the island, just above the water to avoid radar, and arrive at the island just before dawn. Major Weatherly, the squadron CO, was flying lead in the first element. We were to pull up at the last moment and dump our load of parafrags on the parked Zeros—to get in before they knew we were coming, hit them hard, and get the hell out before they could react. At least that was what we were told at the pre-takeoff briefing.

It sounded pretty damned dicey to me, a guy who was on his first combat mission. Not only was it my first combat mission, but I was scheduled to fly as navigator in the lead ship of the second element. Oh sure, I had trained as a DR (dead reckoning) navigator, but I was primarily a bombardier. What the hell was I doing flying as a lead navigator on my first mission?

Moments before takeoff, Major Weatherly strolled over and began to chat with me. I am certain he wanted to make the new guy feel a little less nervous than he had every right to be. He casually asked where I had taken my navigational training. When I told him I was a DR navigator, his jaw dropped as he blurted out—"Geez, what the hell are you doing as a lead navigator?" I meekly told him that I had nothing whatsoever to do with the assignment and that I shared his concern.

He very quickly had me swap places with the navigator on the second ship, a man who was not only a real navigator but a combat veteran as well. I very quietly took the copilot's seat in the second ship and introduced myself to the pilot as his new navigator. He put me somewhat at ease by telling me this would be his 35th mission. It might be a dicey mission, but at least I was going with a seasoned veteran.

The first element took off and we followed in about ten minutes. We were to join with the lead plane while on course, rather than circling the field to join in formation. I gave the pilot the course to steer and away we went. Five minutes passed, then ten, but still no sight of our lead plane.

I glanced at the compass and saw that we were flying five degrees off the course I had given the pilot. I called this to his attention and he immediately came back on course. We continued to search the dark sky for the wing lights of number one, but to no avail. Looking again at the compass, I saw that we were once more five degrees off course. "Bring her back five degrees left," I said to the pilot.

It was time now to arm the parafrags. I slipped out of my parachute and lowered myself into the bomb bay, with flashlight in one hand and pliers in the other. Placing one foot on each bomb bay door, I began the job of pulling the pins from the bombs. Apparently the armament guys wanted to be certain the pins did not come loose accidentally, as they had twisted each pin into such a diabolical configuration that it required my holding the flashlight in my mouth as I used both hands in the attempt to remove the nasty little buggers.

I suddenly realized that my legs were very cold and getting colder by the minute. Looking down, I saw that the bomb bay doors were creeping open from my weight. "Lord Almighty," I thought, "here I am over these G D mountains in the dark of night, with the doors opening, and me with no parachute!" I leaped up to a point where I was able to put a foot on each of two fuselage stringers, as I spanned the bomb bay with my wide-spread legs.

After what seemed an eternity, I finally removed the last pin and heaved a mighty sigh of relief. I scrambled back out of the bomb bay and slid into the navigation compartment, where I sat for several minutes recovering from the shakes before again donning my 'chute.

Then it was back to the copilot's seat and a quick glance at the compass. We were again five degrees off course. I realized that the pilot, in looking out his window to his side as he sought the lead plane, inadvertently moved the wheel slightly to the right. This was just enough to put us off course. At this point, I changed to the follow-the-pilot mode of navigation and recomputed our position.

One degree off course equals one mile off course for every sixty miles of forward progress. We had now been airborne for almost an hour which, at our ground speed, placed us about twenty miles off our planned course. Quite obviously, it would be

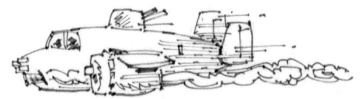

impossible to spot our lead ship unless he too was way off course in the same direction as we were. Weatherly's instructions had been extremely explicit, "No plane is to attack the target solo. If your wing man is not there, do not go in." It was obvious to me that we would soon be returning to Yangkai.

As we continued on our way to Hainan Island, I informed the crew and suggested that they clear their guns. The pilot ripped off a short burst with the nose and package guns. Moments later, I heard the tail gunner cut loose, followed first by one waist gun and then the other. We pressed on in the dark of night.

About five minutes later, the pilot and I almost jumped out of our seats on hearing a tremendous blast of sound immediately overhead. The Plexiglas cockpit cover reverberated wickedly, for all the world like a mighty church bell being rung by some giant Quasimodo.

I damn near dirtied my drawers. "What in the name of all that's holy is going on? Are we under attack?" We were like two kids passing through the town cemetery at the "witching hour" on Halloween night. A single airplane in the dark of night, deep in enemy territory—Who knows what goes bump in the night?—What sort of evil spirit is lurking out there in the dark, just waiting to pounce on us?

Slowly it dawned on us, the engineer/gunner had fired the upper turret with the twin 50's pointed directly forward and directly parallel to the overhead Plexiglas. Why he had waited so long after my telling the crew to clear their guns was a mystery to me.

At this point, the pilot said, "Let's go home. Give me a new course to fly." He salvoed the bombs and made a 180 degree turn. On the return flight there was no deviation from course, as the pilot was no longer looking for the other plane. We hit Yangkai dead center and within one minute of my ETA (estimated time of arrival).

It turned out that the mission was a total flop, insofar as the 22nd was concerned. No one bombed Hainan. Our lead man had pressed on without us, almost reaching Hainan before turning back. He was headed for a landing at Kweilin when he ran out of gas and made a crash landing in a river. A valiant airman was lost and deeply mourned by all in the squadron when the navigator who had taken my place at the last minute drowned in the river.

VIETNAMESE TRAIN CREW SETS NEW RECORD FOR THE 100 METER DASH

It is early April of '44 and I am scheduled to fly as navigator on the lead plane of a two-plane sweep of the China Sea. Although this is but my second combat mission, I feel perfectly at ease as my pilot today is Jim Schooley, a combat veteran of almost 50 missions and one of the smoothest and most experienced of all the 22nd Bomb Squadron pilots.

My first mission had been a bit on the spooky side and had been aborted. It was a "take off in the dark of night and hit them at dawn's early light" strike against a Japanese fighter base on Hainan Island. Now, less than a week after our aborted mission we are headed once more for the South China Sea. This time, the weather couldn't be more beautiful. Not only was this a daylight strike but it was CAVU (ceiling and visibility unlimited) all the way.

Our flight from Yangkai to the sea was like a Sunday drive in the park. We saw no signs of enemy activity. On reaching the open water, we began searching for targets of opportunity, hoping to find a cargo ship or two carrying Japanese supplies. For the first fifteen to twenty minutes, we saw absolutely nothing.

Then, on the horizon, I saw what appeared to be two Japanese navy ships making a high speed turn in our direction. I poked Jim in the arm and pointed to these ships. Jim eyed the ships for a moment or two then grabbed for the mike to call to our wing man, "Looks like we might have a couple of Jap ships down there, let's go get them." With that, he dove for the surface, leveling off at about 100 feet above the water as we bore in on the ships. Unfortunately the "navy ships" turned out to be two large fishing junks trawling nets in the water.

Another half hour or so of patrolling the sea and we gave up and headed for what is now North Vietnam, looking for bridges and rolling stock as targets of opportunity. We located a small railroad bridge a bit northeast of Hanoi and Jim and the other pilot did a number on it, blowing it out of its emplacement. That should put a crimp in the rail traffic for a week or so.

Then it was "press on" again, looking for new targets. Jim finally spotted a locomotive sitting on a spur ready to roll, with steam spewing from its stack. Both planes dove on the locomotive, with our wingman trailing behind Jim.

On spotting us approaching with their destruction in mind, the crew bailed out of the locomotive and streaked for the forest. It was as though the Devil himself was nipping at their keesters as they ran. As a one-time varsity runner, I was positively amazed at their speed.

Jim lined up with the locomotive, aimed and kicked out his 500 pounder. It skipped several times as it approached the locomotive and then in a final skip, it went over the target and into the forest where it exploded. Our wing man had no better luck with his bomb.

Frustrated and hot under the collar, Jim said to me, "Put a high explosive shell in the 75 mm cannon, I'm going to get that SOB." I did as he asked. On our next pass he took very deliberate aim and held off on firing until we were damned near on top of the locomotive. His aim was perfect. The locomotive, belching

steam and heavy smoke, disintegrated into thousands of small parts flying in all directions.

We damned near blew ourselves up as we flew through that mess of swirling, twirling pieces of wreckage. Several of the smaller parts rained down on the fuselage. But Jim had done the job in a glorious manner—he had gotten the SOB! I still think that the engineer and brakeman on that locomotive broke the world's existing record for the 100 meter sprint.

We were all in a pretty happy mood on our return flight to Yangkai. I stood in my navigation compartment looking out through the windscreen and thinking—"Two down and forty eight to go—I can do that standing on my head."

WHOSE SIDE ARE YOU ON?

It is about mid-April, 1944. The Japs are making the strongest effort yet to dislodge the Tigers from China. Our eastern bases were under threat of immediate airborne attack and plans had been formulated for destruction of these bases, coupled with a deployment of all American units to the safer confines of southwest China. General Chennault had dictated there would be no retreat from Yangkai. The base was to be defended at all costs.

Security became the operative word. Slit trenches were dug around the outer perimeter of the base and each of us was assigned a post to occupy should a Japanese attack materialize. As an example, I was assigned to one of the outermost slit trenches. I would be armed with a Thompson machine gun and my Colt 45 pistol. I would be joined by about six enlisted personnel with carbines and 45 pistols. We were to defend against Japanese paratroopers. I figured if we were incredibly fortunate, we might be able to hold out for perhaps as long as five minutes against a dedicated attack by a well-armed, infantry-trained enemy. It goes without saying that most of us were very antsy about the situation but there was little we could do to alleviate the fear.

It was during a dinner hour in a very unsettling time frame that we learned the 22nd would be flying a mission the following day. Crew assignments for the mission were to be posted in the mess hall by 1900 hours. At the appointed hour, Lee Baker and I decided to walk over to the mess hall to see whether or not we were slated to fly. I now had two combat missions under my belt while Lee was still waiting to fly his first.

As we departed our room, I looked skyward to see what the weather might be for the morrow—big mistake—I took about  two or three steps and fell ass over teakettle to the bottom of a newly dug slit trench. There was absolutely no excuse for me to have forgotten about the existence of this particular trench. Days earlier, I had seen it dug by one of our squadron mates who had been a bad boy of one sort or another. As a result of his infraction of the rules, he had been ordered by Zed Barnes to dig the trench as punishment for his crime.

He had dug only about a foot or two in depth when he decided he was having no more of this. Throwing down his shovel, he glared at Barnes and said, "Kiss my ass, I ain't digging no hole and there ain't no way you can make me do it." The major, in a manner later made famous by Clint Eastwood, dropped his hand to his Colt 45 in the holster riding his hip and suggested the man continue digging as ordered.

The alternative seemed crystal clear— "Make my day." There followed a period of several minutes of great tension as each attempted to stare the other down. In the end it was no contest, the man picked up the shovel and didn't put it down again until he had completed digging.

Now, cursing mightily as Baker howled in laughter at his navigator who couldn't navigate more than five feet before encountering disaster, I climbed out of this dark pit and we headed once more for "Kulichkoff's Kafe." Although Baker was not on the flight list, yours truly was. As we exited the mess hall, I scanned the heavens once more and saw a strange sight. A number of fires illuminated the mountaintops on three sides of the airstrip, forming a rather well-defined horseshoe of light. "What do you suppose the natives are up to?" I asked Lee. "Do you think they are having an evening barbecue for all the Chinese in the surrounding area?"

"Beats hell out of me," he replied.

Within an hour or so, we heard, "Three ball alert, head for the hinterland, they're on the way." Moments later as we sat alongside a rice paddy on the village side of the field, we heard the unmistakable, "whomp—whomp—whomp" sound produced by a Betty bomber with engines deliberately out of sync. For what seemed like an eternity, that Nip pilot tooled back  and forth over the field, occasionally dropping a single, poorly aimed bomb.

As I recall, only one of those bombs came close, hitting near the end of the runway but causing no real damage. Most of the bombs fell behind us, much closer to the village of Yangkai than to the airstrip. Although causing no real damage, our Japanese tormentor had succeeded in making us spend several miserable hours crouched in the cold damp night air.

Later that evening, Tokyo Rose spoke of the raid on the air base and went on to identify some of the crew members who would be flying on tomorrow's mission. Mine was one of the names mentioned—talk about spooky—this was highly disturbing and somewhat hair-raising to say the least. Without question, all of these  very strange events were directly related to one another—the fires surrounding the base, the attack of the Betty bomber and Tokyo Rose's knowledge of our planned mission.

The burning question was, "Just who the hell is the Japanese agent at work in Yangkai? Was it one of our trusted house boys? If not, was it one of the mess hall attendants?" Without question, it was someone with access to the mess hall as well as availability of a communication system with which to pass on the information regarding the mission. We never did learn the source of the leak nor, to the best of my recollection, did we ever again have fires surrounding the base and an acknowledgement of our existence by Tokyo Rose.

TAKE ON THE DESTROYERS

How many of you remember the spring of '44 when the U.S. Navy was in hot pursuit of the Japanese fleet, driving it back into the home waters? A large task force of Japanese vessels, including cruisers and escorting destroyers, was reported to be steaming north toward Hainan Island in their flight from our navy. The task force would arrive in the vicinity of Hainan within two days. Whether acting under orders from higher authority or on his own initiative, the "old man" announced an all-out 14th Air Force attack on the task force. The B-24s would bomb the cruisers from high altitude while the three squadrons of B-25s were to launch wave-top attacks on the destroyers.

During my fifty-mission tour with the 22nd Bomb Squadron, this was the only planned mission for which the 341st Bomb Group commander, Colonel "Preacher" Wells, personally conducted the pre-mission briefing. I "lucked out" and drew an assignment as bombardier-navigator on one of the 22nd aircraft that would be making the mission—big thrill! I had flown all of three or four missions at this point and now was scheduled for what seemed to me to be nothing short of a U.S. version of the Kamikaze attacks. We would be coming in at perhaps fifty feet at a speed of no greater than 300 MPH and taking on a destroyer armed with automatic weapons from stem to stern. It was small consolation to know that I would be riding in one of our "H" models sporting the 75 mm cannon.

So we get lucky and get one or two hits in with the 75—big deal. Forget our skip bombing—most of the bombs dropped in this manner skip right over or under the target.

What the hell did the brass think those little nips would be doing as we lumbered toward them? Mother, put a gold star in your window.

Came the morning of the big raid and all of eastern China was socked in with a fantastic storm. The window of opportunity slammed shut and the mission was scrubbed. Who says the man upstairs isn't looking after you?

IF HE'S SPORTING A RADIAL
ENGINE, SHOOT HIM DOWN

It is spring, 1944. I now have a half dozen missions under my belt as a member of the 22nd Bomb Squadron. On this occasion I will be flying as bombardier/navigator on the lead aircraft of a three plane sea sweep to be conducted south of Hainan Island. While any mission can be disastrous, this did not appear to be a particularly high-risk venture. I had been on several other such sea sweeps and had seen nothing other than a few large junks under sail. In those instances we had come back into Indochina and shot up rails and rolling stock while encountering no resistance. We could probably expect more of the same today.

In earlier briefings, we had been told to keep our eyes peeled for radial engine fighters, as all of ours were inline engines. "If its a radial, shoot him down, he's a Jap." This info had been neatly stored away in my memory bank with other trivia. Now we were tooling toward the South China Sea, making small talk as we approached the coast. The weather was beautiful and nothing seemed out of order. Arriving over the water, we began our search.

Suddenly, out of the corner of my eye, in the one o'clock position, I spotted a large flight of what appeared to be fighter  type aircraft. There were at least thirty in number and were approaching at roughly our altitude on a course perpendicular to our own. As they closed on us, I damned near dirtied my drawers—they sported radial engines, and here we sat unescorted and hundreds of miles from friendly territory. Breaking radio silence, I alerted the other aircraft and said a small prayer. After what seemed an eternity, but was probably only a matter of seconds, the big, beautiful American star was spotted on the fuselages. "Hey guys, those are our brown shoe friends from the Yewnited States Navy." Don't know what you're doing here fellas but sure glad to see you! It seems they had launched from a U.S. carrier 50 to 75 miles south of our position and were zeroed in on Hainan Island as their target. We, or at least I, had no inkling that our navy was within a thousand miles of the area.

IT WASN'T OUR TIME

It was May of '44 and the 22nd Bomb Squadron was looking for a replacement for the departed squadron bombardier. In their quest, the brass tried a number of the newer bombardiers. Each would fly as lead bombardier against at least one of a number of selected targets. All bombing would be done from approximately 10,000 feet.

On this day, yours truly was in the hot seat. Six B-25s set out from Yangkai. The target was a riverside supply facility in Mengtz, not too far from Hanoi. I was as nervous as the proverbial cat on a hot tin roof. I must have scanned my bombing tables a dozen times to be sure I had the correct ballistic coefficient for the bombs we were carrying. The proper coefficient would allow me to set the precise amount of trail essential to my calculations. I checked and rechecked the outside temperature, I calculated and recalculated our ground speed—I wanted my pre-set tangent of the dropping angle to be as correct as humanly possible. This would minimize the amount of adjusting required on the rate knobs—this one had to be my very best performance on the old Norden bomb sight.

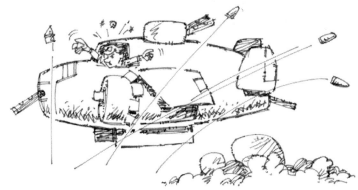

As we approached the IP (initial point), I had rolled in the extended vision and had my right eye glued to the eyepiece. It was a beautiful day without a cloud in the sky. Suddenly, a black cloud appeared ahead and below our position—where in hell had that come from? Moments later a second black cloud mushroomed much closer to our position. Jerking my eye from the eyepiece, I looked at this stranger to determine its origin. At the same moment a third cloud appeared directly below us and I heard a sound like light hail against the fuselage. In that moment, I finally realized what was going on—this was flak and it was too damn close.

Putting my eye back on the eyepiece, I completed the bombing run and we scored very well against the target. Bomb bay doors now closed, we turned tail and headed for Yangkai like a scared horse seeking his stable. The formation tightened up in order to present a smaller target for those Japanese gunners.

I had just started to breathe easier when a fiery object about the size of a basketball zipped between the port engine and the left side of my greenhouse. It was gone in a flash, headed skyward. "What the hell, I must be seeing things," I thought, "no way that could have been real because, if it was, we had been incredibly lucky." It had missed my greenhouse and the port engine by mere inches. I decided to say absolutely nothing to the others on the crew—they would think I was wacky.

After landing at Yangkai, the pilot (whose name I have since forgotten) called me aside for a "mano a mano" chat. He asked, "Did you see anything a little on the scary side just after we left the target area?"

"What do you mean scary?" I asked rather guardedly. I wasn't about to offer any comments on a "mirage." He then told me that I would probably think he was suffering from combat fatigue but he could have sworn that he had seen a bright, fiery object rocketing upward, just inches from my greenhouse and the left engine. To this day, I have no idea as to what it was that came that close to turning this one into our final mission.

The competition continued for several months and culminated in July when I was named squadron bombardier.

TAKE THIS JOB AND SHOVE IT

It was at Yangkai—summer of '44. Because of inclement weather, the 22nd Bomb Squadron had been standing down for a week or so. While sitting in the mess hall, several of us were bitching—"At this rate we will never get in our 50 missions and that beautiful ticket back to the good old you ess of aye." On hearing this, Lieutenant "Mac" McCue, our feisty, bantam rooster communications officer, became almost apoplectic.

"You G D fly boys give me a royal pain in the ..." he roared, "You're a spoiled bunch of prima donnas—sit around on your keister all day, pickle your brains, small as they are, in Jing Bao juice, fly 50 lousy missions and then its back home with a chest full of medals, while we're stuck here for three stinking years."

He was particularly critical of bombardiers. "My heart really bleeds for you buttholes. You sit up in the front with the best seat in the house while someone else chauffeurs you to the target area. The copilot has to damn near knock you off your seat to wake you on arrival—you fiddle with your lousy knobs for a couple of minutes, come out with that corny, 'Bombs away—bomb bay doors closed' bullshit and then sit back and snooze on the ride home—tough damned duty ain't it?"

Somewhat abashed by this totally unexpected tirade, I asked if he would care to join me in the greenhouse on our next mission. "You bet your ... I would," he spit out, "It'll be the easiest three or four hours of my life."

That evening, I told the "old man" of Mac's feelings and asked if I could take him along on our next trip. "By all means," he replied, "I think its a great idea."

As luck would have it, that next mission was the most action-filled I was to experience during my entire tour of duty—close air support for ground troops—not particularly dangerous

275

but a hell of a lot more exciting than bombing from eight to ten thousand feet.

Operating in the mountains about 100 miles or so west of Yunnanyi, a sizable force of Chinese infantry had been pinned down by a small band of Japanese troops. Although fewer than 200 Japs occupied the hilltop, they were wreaking havoc with the friendlies. With deadly cross fire from machine guns, they cut the Chinese down like so much wheat on each of their attempts to storm the hill. After each retreat of the Chinese, the Japs would lob mortar shells down on their position. The Chinese were being cut to ribbons—decimated and with little hope for changing the situation. An urgent call was sent out for close air support.

Six B-25s of the 22nd Bomb Squadron were quickly loaded with frag bombs and dispatched to the scene. Half of the aircraft were J models with the conventional greenhouse. The others were the single-pilot H model, with its 75 mm nose cannon and 8 fixed fifties—ideally suited for close support work.

I was riding in the lead plane, a J model. Mac climbed into the greenhouse with me. He sat on a small wooden box as I assumed my usual position on the ammo canister. There would be no bombing for me today, as this was going to be skip bombing at tree top level. My role this day was simply that of nose gunner using the single, flexible, fifty caliber machine gun which was mounted in the greenhouse.

As we neared Yunnanyi, two P-40's joined up and led us to the target area. Once there, they peeled off and marked the hilltop with smoke rockets, firing as they did so. At this point, the fun began. Diving in single file, the B-25s screamed toward the hill top at about 300 per. As the ground rushed toward us, Mac's color began to fade a bit. Once in range, all hell broke loose. The pilot began firing the four pod-mounted fifties. The twin fifties in the top turret cut loose with a vengeance and I was blasting away with the flex fifty. The din was unbelievable. Within seconds, the greenhouse was filled with acrid smoke and the stench of cordite. At this point, the pilot punched out the frags and immediately put the plane into a gut-wrenching, screaming chandelle to the left.

By the time we leveled off, Mac was positively green. Looking back at the target area as the second B-25 made his pass, we saw Jap troops stand and fire at him as he passed overhead. The decision was made to launch two strafing passes following the frag bombing.

When the last plane cleared the target area we commenced our first strafing run. With earphones clamped tight over my 100-

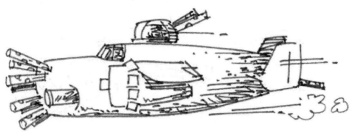

mission hat and a butt dangling out of my mouth as I stood hosing the area with the 50, I was the typical WWII "B" movie character personified. By now the remaining Japs were desperate enough that they were sporadically returning our machine gun fire as we approached their position. As I was firing, Mac casually asked what those white balls zipping through the air might be. "Tracers, old buddy," I replied, "They're shooting back"—dead silence from Mac.

On our third and final pass, although there was no longer any firing from the ground, I felt a pressure on my shoulders and spine but was too busy firing to investigate. After we cleared the area, I looked back. Mac, with both hands on my shoulders and eyes tightly closed, had his head buried against my back—perhaps he thought I might be able to deflect any slugs headed our way.

I could fully appreciate his trepidation, probably thinking, "Here I am in the nose of a goddamn airplane, with nothing but glass all around me, zipping over the tree tops at 300 MPH; some mean-minded little sumbitch on the ground is trying to part my skull with a machine gun slug, and me without even a rock in my hand to chuck back at the bastard."

On our return to Yangkai, Mac leaped from the plane, threw himself to his knees and kissed the ground several times. When I asked if he would care to do it again he said, "Screw you guys and your stinking airplanes, I'll stick to my radios."

We later learned the Chinese had been able to amble up the hill without a shot being fired at them—there were no Jap survivors. Never again did we hear a single word about the idyllic life of the fly-boy. Nor, I must add, did I ever admit to Mac that much of what he had said about bombardiers was right on the money.

KISS YOURSELF GOODBYE

It was the summer of 1944. The 22nd Bomb Squadron based at Yangkai had established Tingkwak Sakan, Burma, as a staging site for missions in support of the Burma campaign. Carved out of the Burmese jungles, Tingkwak was about as primitive a base as existed in the CBI. Get five feet into the surrounding jungles and it would have been impossible to see a convoy passing by. Quarters were tents spread out under the towering canopies of rain forest trees. Heavy mist or fog hung over the area until ten or eleven a.m. Monkeys by the hundreds swung through the trees overhead, screaming and dropping excrement as they traversed the area. Boots were shaken vigorously before donning to dislodge any scorpion that might have taken up residence over the night. In short, it was a "Shangri La."

On occasion, the 22nd would hit a target in Burma, land at Tingkwak, and then fly a second mission on the return to Yangkai. I had recently been named as squadron bombardier. On this occasion, we were given a target to strike in Burma, probably Myitkyina, after which we were to land at and stay overnight in Tingkwak. Intelligence had reported that the Japs were using the Burma Road during night-time hours for moving personnel and supplies. It was decided that on our return mission from Tingkwak we would seed the road with bombs armed with delayed action fuses set to detonate during those night-time hours when it was said that the Japanese were active on the road.

During the pre-mission briefing, I was told that the armament people at Yangkai would install the fuses overnight to be sure of their readiness. We would then take off the next morning with our regular bomb load aboard for the first mission. I would be given the delayed action fuses for our return mission. When I questioned, "Why me?" I was told that armament had no personnel at Tingkwak at the time and that it would be up to me as squadron bombardier to

279

fuse the bombs for the return mission. Then came the bad news. These little gems were each equipped with an anti-removal device. I was instructed to supervise the loading of all bombs in the six aircraft and then to disperse all other squadron personnel to the jungles while I installed the fuses. Should a fuse be installed in a cross threaded manner, I was to lower the bomb very gently and move it deep into the jungle for demolition. The reason for these instructions was immediately apparent—better to lose one bombardier than 60 or 70 men and six aircraft. One quarter turn counter-clockwise and I could kiss my ... goodbye.

Needless to say, I slept very little the night before takeoff. I could envision myself attempting to align the threads on the fuses, perhaps ten inches or more inside the extended bomb fins, with hands shaking like those of a 95 year old with palsy. I could see the story in the Detroit News, "Local boy blown to hell in the jungles of Burma." Following breakfast (which I  almost upchucked), I reported to operations only to be told that the road seeding mission had been scrubbed. Praise the Lord!

THE WOES OF A BOMBARDIER

It was one of those ho-hum missions to a walled-in Japanese supply depot near some long since forgotten village in French Indochina. The target area was probably about 400 feet wide by 1,000 feet long—tailor-made for a bombardier who had been on a roll for the last half dozen or so strikes.

No opposition was expected nor was any encountered. It was as though the six B-25s from the 22nd were out for a leisurely stroll. Sitting in the greenhouse as squadron bombardier, I felt particularly confident. Don Tewes, our intelligence officer, was sharing the greenhouse with me. Don was one of those unusual intelligence types who preferred to ride along on our combat missions, thereby allowing him to assess, first-hand, our effectiveness.

The Norden was well warmed up and I had computed and recomputed the tangent of the dropping angle and the amount of trail to be set in for the bombs we carried. On our approach, I even engaged the extended vision knob, thereby enabling me to crank in our initial drift. This was going to be my best ever. My first bomb was to drop 50 feet short of the nearest wall to compensate for the delay caused by the other bombardiers waiting to see my first bomb before toggling their own. All intervalometers were set to give us 1,000 feet of coverage in range. Bombs away!—crouched next to each other, Don and I were peering through the glass, waiting for that first burst of smoke. Suddenly it appeared—right on the money, in range but about 400 feet left of the left wall. We watched in disbelief and dismay as every bomb from the formation struck outside the wall.

281

Based on our altitude, it was obvious that I was off by half a bubble length in deflection. I would like to believe that the reason for the error was the fact that the airplane was not level, when the pilot told me it was, during my bubble leveling operation. Bill Prudler would no doubt dispute that allegation and, I suspect, with good reason. In all probability, my cockiness led to sloppiness.

In any event, on our return to base, Major Nickels, our C.O., asked Tewes for his report. Without cracking a smile and with a voice of authority, Don reported that we had been 66-2/3% accurate. Somewhat puzzled by this response, the good major asked Don for amplification of this rather amazing preciseness of assessment. Without changing his serious demeanor, Tewes stated that he was giving White 33-1/3% for hitting Asia and an additional 33-1/3% for hitting French Indochina. He concluded by stating that without Newton and Norden, White could not hit the ground.

On another day, we went on a mission to that same walled-in supply depot that I had missed so miserably on the earlier mission. Again, there was perfect weather. The six aircraft proceeded without incident to the target area. As in the last case, Don Tewes, the intelligence officer, was sharing the greenhouse with me.

This time, the results were totally different. Every single bomb was on target. The damage we wreaked was unmistakable. Don was so excited that he asked if we could go back over the target to enable him to take pictures. Feeling vindicated and in an expansive mood, I readily agreed. Getting on the intercom, I asked the pilot to take us back over the top once again. Wanting still more pictures, Don asked if we could do it one more time. Back we went on what was now our third pass over the target. Satisfied that we had done an outstanding job, we headed for home. The return flight was smooth and without incident.

As I climbed out of the front hatch, I saw the rear hatch open almost explosively and T/Sgt. Les Sejarto, our radio operator, spilled out with a wild look on his face. Coming toward me on a dead run, he was waving an object above his head. As he neared, I could see that it was a mess kit, but unlike any other I had seen—it had no bottom—just a ragged hole. Coming to a skidding halt, his red face inches from my own, he screamed, "G... D... it, who in the hell decided to go back over the target?"

Somewhat nonplused, I told him that it had been my decision. Glaring at me, he said, "You son-of-a-bitch—Sir. Look at this," brandishing the mess kit under my nose. Still puzzled, I asked what his problem was. It seems that while on our initial run, his mess kit was sitting on top of the radio. Unknown to any of the others in the crew, a piece of flak had come through the belly of the airplane, blasting the radio and Les' mess kit before exiting. Even as I asked the question, I knew why he had not told us we were under fire—his intercom was lost with the radio. I often think of poor old Les sitting back there knowing we were the target of ground fire while some dopey bombardier was insisting on overflying the area several more times—Sorry, Les, old friend.

TIGER CUBS

A momentous occasion in the life of a tiger cub is that first venture away from the lair without Mama.

The crew of Lt. Leo C. Baker, including Sgts. Les Sejarto, Joe Christofanelli and Allison Carroll along with yours truly, Jim White (bombardier-navigator) took those first tenuous steps on the 15th of April, '44. Actually, I had logged two missions earlier in the month but still considered myself a cub along with the others. We had trained together for months in the states on the B-25 H model and had become as one with the airplane. Lee Baker was probably the best 75 mm gunner in the air force, a factor which was to weigh heavily before the day was over.

The target this day was a railroad bridge some 15 to 20 miles northeast of Hanoi. Two elements of two aircraft each were assigned to the target. The first element, led by Lt. Feigley, took off about 15 minutes before Lt. Bullard's second element. Lt. Weber and crew were flying with Lt. Feigley while we were with Lt. Bullard. Weather was abominable—rain, sleet, hail and heavy turbulence were to plague us throughout the mission. Shortly after passing over the Indochina border we encountered cumulous clouds that extended several thousand feet above our altitude.

Baker turned 45 degrees to the right and climbed until we broke out on top. By now, back on our original course, we were unable to locate Lt. Bullard. Baker looked at me and said, "What do we do now, coach?" Having no better answer I suggested we press on to the target. Our strategy was simple, fly a southerly course until we can spot the river and then just follow it east to the bridge.

Cloud cover below us was at least six to seven tenths. Finally, spotting the river through a hole in the clouds, Baker started our tight, spiraling descent. The pucker factor was high as we knew the valley through which the river flowed to be no more than two to three miles wide with mountains rising on both sides. From time to time, the clouds  completely obscured our vision. It was cold in the cockpit but, looking over at Lee, I could see beads of sweat running off his nose. As for me, I could feel a steady stream running the length of my spine.

We broke into the clear at an altitude of about 800 feet above the valley. From this vantage point, the mountains looming into the clouds on either side of us were truly ominous.

Proceeding down river, we spotted our target that was readily identified by the presence of a very tall, white smokestack on the eastern side of the bridge. As we approached, we observed a number of civilians crossing the bridge. Firing a burst of 50 calibers to clear the bridge, we decided to make two bombing passes, dropping two 1,000 pound bombs on each pass. Ground fire from two positions was encountered. One position, situated on the mountainside next to the bridge, appeared to be a rapid-firing, multi-cannon type antiaircraft installation. The second was a machine gun emplacement located in a small shack on the bridge proper.

With tracers whistling past us, Baker put the aircraft into a screaming chandelle to the left, leveling out at 1,500 feet. We then started our second pass, intending to bomb from 75 feet. I had loaded a high explosive shell into the 75 mm cannon. From a range of about 1/2 mile, Baker took aim at the mountainside and fired. His aim was perfect as the whole installation went up in a tremendous blast.

Now, completing his turn, Lee pointed his nose at the bridge and came in at 75 feet, eyes glued to the skip bomb sight. The ground machine gun position, now dead ahead, was firing at us with a vengeance.

Reaching over from my position, I hit the firing button for our eight, fixed 50 calibers. Seeing what I was up to, Baker kicked first right and then left rudder, spraying our ammo over a wider range. We watched the tracers as they marched up the rails toward the shack. In a flash, that installation too was destroyed. Baker dropped the first two bombs that, because of our maneuvering, sailed harmlessly into the river.

On our third and final pass, we had the area totally to ourselves. Taking very precise aim, Lee released the remaining bombs. Bingo! He had taken out one span and seriously damaged the other. Without waiting for kudos he said, "Let's get the Hell out of here."

Lt. Bullard had experienced loss of power and altitude and had returned to base when we first became separated. The first element had obviously targeted a bridge other than the one we hit. They too came under very heavy ground fire, with both aircraft being hit. The plane piloted by Lt. Weber was heavily damaged. Lt. Weber was seriously wounded while Lt. Thayer, the navigator, sustained lesser wounds. A roving combat photographer had accompanied Lt. Weber's crew on this mission. A civilian pilot, he had actually flown the aircraft for a brief period while Lt. Weber was being treated. Written by the photographer, an account of this mission appeared in Saturday Evening Post under the title "Our Incredible Ride Home."

Needless to say, the brass of the 22nd Bomb Squadron were highly skeptical when told of our results. "A bunch of tiger cubs mounting a one-plane attack and destroying a bridge and two gun emplacements? Ridiculous!"

It was only after Photo Joe and his trusty P-38 came back with confirming pictures that we were given credit for the success. The cubs had become Flying Tigers.

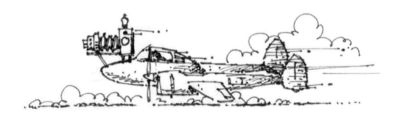

Details of this mission were included in the official history of the 22nd Bomb Squadron which was sent to the Air Force Office of History, Bolling AFB. Lt. Weber was recommended for award of the Silver Star for this mission.

COUNTDOWN TO OBLIVION

In what is to be the second and last time flying together on a mission, the stateside crew of Lee Baker is gathered in a revetment loading the plane with today's bombs. The target is a concentration of ground troops and the bombs are parafrags.

As any bombardier or armament man knows, these little jewels are armed only after the aircraft is airborne. The individual grenade-type bomblets in this particular configuration are secured in a cluster around a central pipe or tube by what looks for all the world like baling wire. The tube contains a 45 caliber slug that is delay-fired after the bomb is dropped from the rack. Passage of the slug severs the baling wire and the bomblets are released individually.

The actual arming occurs only after individual arming propellers on the bomblets rotate about 200 revolutions. This means the bomblet has fallen several hundred feet below the aircraft before becoming live.

Lee Baker is kicking tires, checking the pitot tube (air speed indicator) and doing all those little things that pilots feel are necessary. Joe Christofanelli, the engineer/gunner, and Allison Carroll, the tail gunner, stand next to the airplane shooting the breeze.

Les Sejarto, the radio/gunner, is helping me with the bomb loading. We have placed about four clusters in the racks and reach for a fifth. I notice the wire is extremely rusty—obviously very old bombs. Just as we heave the cluster to chest height, one of the wires breaks and bomblets begin to fall on the tarmac. Cursing mightily, I crawl from beneath the bomb bay to survey the damage. Not a soul in sight. Within several minutes, one-by-one, the heads of my mates appeared over the top of the revetment. "What the hell are you guys doing up there?" I shout.

Obviously they think the bombs are armed and about to explode. Sejarto, last to materialize, responds, "I wasn't about to stay down there and be blown up with you."

Assured that everything is under control, he ambles over the top and down into the revetment, clutching a bomblet tightly to his chest.

TENT CITY AT YUNNANYI

There were two periods of time when I was absent from lovely downtown Yangkai for a month or more. The first was for a period of about five weeks during which I was camped out at Malir, India, with "Whispering Ray" Bohannon and W. O. Powell. We returned to Yangkai during the waning days of June, 1944.

My second straying from the striving metropolis of Yangkai took place in the early fall of 1944, when a large number of crews from the 22nd deployed to "Tent City" on the abandoned fighter strip at Yunnanyi. I no longer recall the duration of this stay but I do recall that I flew some 20 or more missions while I was there.

We returned to Yangkai in January, '45, shortly after I completed my 50th mission. While in Yunnanyi, I occupied the tent immediately alongside that of "Doc" Robert E. Buck and the mission booze and directly across the dirt street from the tent of Joe Rosencrantz and Mickey Spinelli—two of the greatest "moonlight requisitioners" it ever was my pleasure to know.

THE MAN WHO
DREAMED OF TOWER POWER

It was the fall of 1944. The 22nd Bomb Squadron was staging out of an abandoned fighter strip located a mile or so from the Air Transport Command (ATC) base at Yunnanyi. Takeoff and landing instructions were handled by the ATC tower personnel. Lt. McCue, our communications officer, was chafing at the bit.

Life in "Tent City" was bad enough under the best of circumstances, but to be forced to so live while having no real job to perform is intolerable. Sitting in his tent one day, he was deep in thought. Suddenly, leaping to his feet, he shouted, "Eureka, I have found the answer!—I shall build my own tower and it shall be a wondrous thing to behold."

Within an hour, aided and abetted by several hammer-swinging, saw-wielding assistants, Mac was at it. Picking a spot immediately next to the runway, they created indeed a thing of beauty. Soaring some ten feet above the ground, it was crowned by a wooden platform with an area of at least twenty square feet. A ladder built of the finest used two by fours provided Mac with regal access to his throne. Next came the equipment: a transmitter with a peak output of at least two watts and receiver with a sensitivity to match any of today's $5.95 portables. As I recall the antenna, it was an engineering marvel. Fashioned from two straightened clothes hangers and secured to the tower, with a triumphant look on his face, Mac mounted the tower and stood erect, head on high, chest out. He was, without question, Hannibal reincarnated, straddling the highest Alp.

During the next mission briefing, Mac addressed the pilots. In his finest Lincolnesque manner he proclaimed, "Men, you are now free—no more shall you be forced to take orders from the landed gentry of ATC (Air Transport Command), for I had a dream and that dream is now a reality—as of today, we have our own tower." Citing the appropriate frequencies, he directed all pilots to contact him on return from mission.

Several hours later, the three B-25s neared Yunnanyi. Acting on Mac's orders, each pilot in turn attempted contact with Mac, now positioned on his tower. No joy—the return airwaves were silent. Following several attempts, the pilots assumed that Mac had given up and they turned their thoughts to their landings.

For several weeks, the pilots had been demonstrating that tactical approaches were not the sole domain of the fighter jocks.

With each succeeding mission, the flight would overfly the runway at an ever lower altitude. The left wing man would then pull up in a sharp chandelle to the left, dropping his landing gear as he did so. Within seconds, the lead ship would emulate the formation maneuver.

On this particular day, the formation was not much more than five feet off the ground on approach. Standing atop his tower, arms frantically waving, Mac was terrified, and with good cause—with eyes glued to the man on their left, the pilots were totally oblivious to Mac, with the right wingman zeroed in on him, Mac leaped from the tower seconds before the right wing passed over his tower with about four feet to spare.

By morning, the "tower" was gone and once again we were returned to the warm embrace of ATC.

DOWN THE HATCH

Fall 1944. A large number of 22nd Bomb Squadron crews have been staging out of Yunnanyi, placing us much closer to our targets in Burma. Missions are shorter in duration but are also flown with much greater frequency. Quite often, the squadrons will strike one target, land at a remote strip in Burma, reload and bomb another target on return to Yunnanyi.

On this particular day, the weather is raw and cold and the temperature in the greenhouse (the bombardier's compartment) is hovering around 25 to 30 degrees. Flying as squadron bombardier, I am scanning for the target. Because of low hanging clouds, we are unable to see the ground.

Fuel is of no concern as we have been airborne for only two hours at most. The decision is made to orbit the target area in the hope that the clouds below will dissipate. Quite obviously, I cannot leave my station as mine is the only bomb sight in the formation.

Suddenly, I realize my "bombardier's bladder" has let me down. The more I think of it, the worse the situation becomes. The icy chill of my compartment coupled with the inability to move has increased pressure to the agony level—PLEASE—let me at that relief tube. But this is not to be.

Finally, after what seems to be hours, the cloud bank rolls out and there is our target. The bomb sight had long been readied so it is now just a matter of making our run. Crosshairs centered and glued to my aiming point, I watch as the indices meet and the bombs drop.

Not even waiting to see the results, I turn the bomb sight off, close the bomb bay doors and head for that wonderful little tube in the nearby navigator's compartment.

Grabbing for the funnel as I unzip, I notice that both pilots are grinning—let them laugh—I have to go so bad that an amused audience doesn't bother me in the least.

In a moment, the funnel overflows my hand. I know there is a great deal of pressure behind the stream but this is ridiculous. Standing on the step to the pilot's compartment, I stretch the hose. Still an overflow. At this point, I move up to the pilot's deck and stretch the hose to its maximum. There is no way I can stop the flow and still it is slopping over. By now, both pilots are roaring with laughter. To hell with it; slamming the hose down, I proceed to finish by spraying the hatch.

It is at this point that the pilots tell me of their earlier similar experiences. Seems some wag had stuffed the orifice of the relief tube at the point where it exits the fuselage.

THE STRANGLING MAN

It is said that drinking to inebriation brings out the real inner man. Some become boisterous, others combative and eager for a bar-room brawl. Some merely drop off to sleep. I was the world's greatest lover—or so I thought. Perhaps the strangest of all drunks I ever encountered was a tall and rather gangly navigator who, for obvious reasons, I shall call "Ray." He was the consummate loner. Within several months of his arrival in Yangkai, he began to attempt strangulation of any squadron mate who might be handy when the Jing Bao juice had taken its toll.

One incident in particular stands out in my memory. On this occasion, Eddie Sevajian, a short, slender bombardier, was Ray's intended victim. Rocking back and forth on his heels, Ray stared intently at Eddie for several moments. Suddenly, and without a word, he lurched forward and seized him by the throat.

Pandemonium broke out. Others in the room scrambled to break up the attack as Eddie screamed in terror and with good cause—Ray towered above him, face contorted into the mask of a maniacal killer as he attempted to throttle his victim. On the following morning, Ray professed to having absolutely no recollection of the incident. There were several subsequent attacks, but the names of Ray's later victims have escaped my memory.

We move now to the fall of '44, when about half of the 22nd is staging out of Yunnanyi. As luck would have it, Ray becomes one of my tent mates. We are flying shuttle missions against targets in Burma. Taking off from Yunnanyi, we hit the target and then land at Tingkwak Sakan, Burma. We grab a quick bite to eat as our aircraft are refueled and reloaded with bombs and then it's back in the air once again to strike the target a second time before returning to Yunnanyi. I had flown 14 combat missions in seven days time and was bone tired.

297

On completion of the 14th mission, following de-briefing, I headed to my tent. There, standing in the door blocking my entrance, was good old Ray—drunker than a skunk and teetering back and forth on his heels. I flipped him a wave and said, "Hi Ray," and then asked that he step aside to allow me to enter. He simply stared at me in silence, eyes somewhat glazed. Then, without warning, he staggered forward and grabbed for my throat. I was both annoyed and surprised.

At six one and 190 pounds, I was by far his biggest would-be victim. Having little patience for his nonsense, I decided to give him a short grazing right hook to the jaw. I let fly, holding my fist somewhat in check to avoid full contact—I missed. Drawing back, I let go once more in a wider arc. Once again I had miscalculated as my fist landed flush on the button and he dropped like a sack of flour. I called to one of my tent mates and we carried him inside and dumped him rather unceremoniously on his cot. My tent mate very wisely confiscated Ray's 45.

Moments later, shaking his head, he staggered to his feet and glared at me. We were separated by about six feet, with the glowing red hot stove standing between us. Suddenly, he threw a punch although standing at least two yards from my position. Stumbling, he fell against the stove and we heard a sickening hiss as his bare flesh made contact with the stove. Cursing, he stumbled back to his cot and began a search. Turning back to me, mouth twisted in total rage he said, "You bastards took my gun but you forgot this," brandishing his long jungle knife as he spoke. He then told me he would wait until I fell asleep at which time he would, "Carve your heart out." At this point, he positioned himself on his cot, head propped up with one hand while the other grasped the sinister looking knife.

Dead tired but unsure as to what his next move might be, I slid my 45 from the holster. Turning my back to him, I quickly unloaded the weapon and then sat on the edge of my own cot. Now facing him, I pointed the gun in his direction and said, "Ray, we are friends and squadron mates but believe me, I will give you a third eye if you so much as take a single step in my direction." I really had no idea as to what I would do should he attack. Moments before the light was turned off, he was still in that same position glaring at me and brandishing the knife as I lay on  my back, wide awake, with my 45 grasped tightly in my right hand as it rested on my chest.

After what seemed an eternity, I finally slipped into a fitful sleep. On waking in the morning, I immediately looked across the tent. Ray was face down fast asleep. The knife had fallen to the floor in front of him. When he finally awoke it was as though he had no memory whatsoever of the previous evening. His only comment was, "How did I get this bruise on my jaw and how in the hell did I burn my arm so badly?" Within a few days, he was shipped stateside. Perhaps that had been his real goal throughout this strange odyssey.

FUN AND GAMES
IN YUNNANYI

January 1945—Tent City, Yunnanyi. A large contingent from the 22nd Bomb Squadron has been staging missions from an abandoned fighter strip located about two miles from the Air Transport Command (ATC) base. Under the command of Lt. Col. Main, now squadron C.O., the air strikes were directed primarily against targets in Burma.

"Doc" (Robert E.) Buck, the Flight Surgeon, occupied the tent adjacent to mine and his only tent mate was the mission booze. Diagonally, across the dirt road from our tent, were two of the greatest "moonlight requisitioners" it has ever been my pleasure to know. Making frequent raids on the ATC base, Joe Rosenkrantz and Mickey Spinelli constantly showed up with canned hams, canned turkey and other goodies, which they very generously shared with others. No questions were asked and no explanations were offered.

Joe was a big husky Texan who at one time apparently had been a boxer. Mickey, much smaller, was a fast talker in keeping with his Brooklyn background. These were two great guys—salt of the earth.

As time wore on, the air became charged with tension. We were on the go constantly. During one seven day period, I flew 14 missions.

It was just as bad for the others. From time to time, fights broke out—a goodly number of which involved officers. One in particular stands out in my mind. Spilling into the street in front of our tent, Capt. Stephens, our engineering officer, and Lt. Jackson, a bombardier, were having it out. Jackson, with Stephens flat on his back, was getting the best of this one. Suddenly, Lt. McCue, our communications officer, burst from the

tent and leaped on Jackson saying, "You can't do that to my buddy."

Jackson flung Mac to the ground alongside Stephens and began pummeling both.

At this point, Col. Main arrived on the scene and ordered Jackson to cease and desist. Without missing a blow, Jackson retorted, "Keep out of this, colonel, or you're next." Within minutes, the sound and fury had subsided and the combatants returned to their tents.

The next morning, Col. Main directed our adjutant, Captain Pat Trimble, to put Jackson on a plane and get him out of Yunnanyi. Within an hour, Pat and Jackson Jeeped toward a waiting aircraft.

Hours passed with no sign of old Trimble. Finally, several hours past noon, Pat was heard singing in an off-key manner as he weaved his way back to the tents.

Some of the more cynical among us came to the conclusion

that Jackson had successfully raided "Doc" Buck's booze stash and having a jug or two left, when boarding the aircraft, he graciously donated these to Pat Trimble.

PREDESTINATION

Throughout the fall of '44, fully half of the 22nd had been operating out of the tent city of Yunnanyi, China. We had staged a series of missions to Burma that had us all weary and on edge.

We returned to Yangkai in late December '44 or early January '45. I had completed 50 missions with visions of returning stateside in February. When the list of returnees was released, my name was among the missing. Thunderstruck, I cornered Pat Trimble with a demand for an explanation. Pat told me I had been put in for promotion to captain, which entailed a two month extension on tour. All of this was news to me. Pat then asked if I would rather go home in February thereby foregoing the promotion. There was no question as to my preference. I hadn't seen my wife in a year and I had a 9 month old daughter whom I had never seen, as she was born three months after my arrival in China. Pat assured me that there would be no problem. My name  would be removed from the promotion list but was submitted too late to make the returnee list. I was furious.

When the time came for our returnees to enplane for Kunming, I would not even go down to see them off.

Then came the horrible news. Traveling in a group, all of our returnees were on a plane headed from Chabua to Karachi when, for reasons never determined, the plane slammed into a mountainside near Tibet.

With one single miraculous exception, all aboard were killed. T/Sgt. Marvin Jacobs was thrown clear and suffered nothing more than a broken ankle and severe shock. He was rescued by Tibetan natives who took him to a local village where he remained for two weeks until two army men parachuted in to build a temporary  strip for a rescue aircraft. Ten days later, he was moved to a hospital in India.

Others from the 22nd who lost their lives on that fateful flight included: Lts. Myron Cook; John McDonough, Jr.; Lewis Werland; James Brokaw; John Flach; Harold Morse and Marshall Young. Also, Sgts. Allan Cousins; Philip Feld; Robert Finks; Lawrence Jacobs; Harlan Gasner; Alva Floyd; Joseph Hewitt, Jr.; Merrill Hyde; Ernest Schenk and Foreman Smith.

We were devastated by this horrendous accident. Seventeen close friends, room-mates, comrades-in-arms wiped out in one blinding flash. To have come through China unscathed only to die while returning home, and to loved ones, was almost more than we could accept.

On my returning to the States during March '45, we stopped in India and visited with Marv Jacobs. I was amazed at his buoyant air considering the ordeal he had survived. But perhaps that is the key. Marv is a survivor by nature. I spoke to him by phone in recent times—our first contact in more than 40 years. He still had that upbeat note in his voice.

LET'S TAKE A WALK
ON THE WILD SIDE

Mid-April, 1944. The 22nd has no mission this day so Lee Baker and I decide to take a stroll in the countryside in the general vicinity of Yangkai. Before starting our walk, we stopped by the armament office and loaded up on 45 caliber ammo for our side arms. We were told we could have as much as we wanted as long as we were willing to strip them from a large number of Thompson machine gun clips stored in the building. We each took about 50 rounds.

Our walk took us into the woods about five miles from the base. It was very quiet and peaceful under the trees. We hadn't seen a single native for at least an hour. We finally came across a small creek—great spot for some shooting. We set up a man-sized target on the bank of the creek, which we then fired on from a distance of about 50 yards. A few shots allowed us to determine the trajectory from that range. We found we could place our rounds in the chest area by aiming a foot or so above the target.

We had been shooting for about 15 minutes when we heard bells tinkling in the distance. From the Doppler effect, it was apparent they were nearing our location. We finally saw the source—a column of about 50 very rough looking, gimlet-eyed men, heavily armed and riding pony sized horses. They were not wearing military uniforms, thus ruling out the possibility that this was a Chinese army unit. Behind each man was a heavily laden supply pony festooned with a bell. It was the bells that we heard.

Each man wore two bandoleers of ammo and had a rifle strapped across his back. They stared at us in stony silence. Nor was there any of the thumbs up and "ding hao" greeting we had come to expect from the natives.

By now, I was sweating bullets and the pucker factor was at an all-time high. The thought raced through my mind, *Hope to hell these aren't the infamous Chinese bandits we had heard of from time to time. Wouldn't it be a hell of a note for the two of us to have gone through all that training as aviation cadets followed by months of operational training in the states only to be knocked off by bandits before we had a chance to contribute to the war effort?*

When they finally passed without incident, both of us heaved huge sighs of relief. We came to the conclusion that this had been either a detachment of Mao Tse Tung's Chinese Communist party army or else a local guerilla outfit on the move.

Having lost all interest in our target area, we moved on. After about 15 minutes of walking, we heard shots from a position ahead of us. We now crouched down and attempted to close in on this source of firing without being spotted. On topping a rise, we found we were on the outskirts of a Chinese army camp. The shooting was coming from the rifle range. We now stood erect and approached the camp. We walked over to the range and watched the proceedings. Some 25 or more Chinese army recruits in ill-fitting uniforms were lying in a prone position, about 50 yards from individual targets.

These very young men could well have been rice farmers conscripted by the local warlord. That seemed to be a very common practice in the Chinese army of the WWII era. Armed with ancient Enfield rifles, each of these shooters had what was apparently an instructor draped over his body. The instructor would aim over the student's shoulder and then clap the student on the back. This was apparently a signal for the student to fire. When the bullet completely missed the target, as they invariably did, the instructor would slap the bee jabbers out of the student and then repeat the entire process once more. It was pretty obvious to us why it was possible for a small band of Japanese soldiers to kick hell out of a much larger Chinese force.

Our presence at the range did not go unnoticed. A widely grinning Chinese lieutenant using very rudimentary sign language invited us to fire our Colt 45's at the targets. The entire Chinese cadre was amazed to see these two "megwas" (Chinese for "Americans") placing one shot after another in the heart section of their targets, using nothing more than pistols. We stayed for perhaps a half hour before returning to base.

RANK HAS ITS PRIVILEGES

It is early May of 1944 and, with only a half dozen or so missions under my belt, I have been named as one of the 22nd Bomb Squadron officers to report to Malir, India, for training on the 75 mm cannon. It seems somewhat redundant to me inasmuch as I have already undergone extensive training with the cannon while at Columbia, S.C. But mine was "not to reason why." I dutifully packed for a stay of about 3 to 4 weeks and went to the airstrip to board a flight to Kunming.

The following day, I wangled passage on an Air Transport Command C-47 bound for Bangalore. In all, we probably had 15 to 20 passengers on the flight, none of whom I knew. The senior passenger was a full colonel. This guy apparently took a liking to me and conferred upon me the nickname "Slim." For what reasons, which will become apparent to the reader, I have given him the pseudonym "Jack Carter."

Jack was extremely loquacious. He told me he was a demolition expert and had just completed the destruction of the 11th Bomb Squadron's air base at Kweilin, with a Japanese invasion force then just several miles from the base.

He told a wild tale of fleeing the area by Jeep and then making his way to Kunming where he had given his report to General Chennault and staff. I knew  we had been told the Japanese were going to push us out of China if possible but was not aware of any action at Kweilin. This was news to me but, having no reason to question the story, I simply congratulated him on his success. A big man, he was extremely believable. Although not at all a John Wayne look-alike, he was the "Duke" personified in his mannerisms.

311

We chatted for the entire flight before landing at Chabua, India, for refueling. Once on the ground, our pilot, a major, told us to remain at or very near the plane as he would be taking off immediately following the refueling. He emphasized his position by stating he would leave without any passenger foolhardy enough to stray from the plane. Jack looked at me and said, "Hey, Slim, let's go to the mess hall and get a cup of Joe and perhaps a donut."

"Gosh, colonel," I said, "I think we had better stay right here—you know what the major said about leaving AWOL passengers behind." With a mile wide grin on his face, Jack asked if I really believed the major had the guts enough to dump a bird colonel. I stuttered and stammered and said something about the fact that I was only a lowly lieutenant and that the major would have no problem whatsoever doing as he wished with me. Jack grinned once more and told me that he was ordering me to accompany him.

On our return about a half hour later, the major was livid. He said not a word to Jack but advanced on me. Face red and twisted in rage, he chewed me out as I had never before been chewed. I could only mutter something about being ordered by the colonel to leave with him. The major thundered, "But I ordered you to stay at the plane."

"Yes, sir," I replied, "but he is a full colonel." The major gave me a withering look and ordered me, "Get your ass on the plane."

On our arrival in Bangalore, Jack asked where I was staying for the night. I told him I had no idea but would look for a transient BOQ. He said, "Like hell, you can stay with me at the Air Technical Service Command (ATSC) facilities—a hell of a lot better than some seedy old BOQ." With that he walked up to the desk at the airport and ordered the sergeant on duty to get him a car (no driver) and to make reservations for the two of us at the

ATSC. The sergeant was told that I was on assignment to the colonel who was a member of the ATSC.

In due course, an olive drab Ford sedan was delivered to Jack and away we went with him driving. He obviously knew the city of Bangalore. Following a short drive, we arrived in a shabby section of the city. Jack pulled up in front of a building and told me to wait for him. With that, he bolted into the building. He returned about 15 minutes later with a look of great pleasure on his face. From his remarks, it was apparent his hormones had been raging before our stopping.

Next it was a tea plantation just outside town. Here I met a very attractive looking British woman who greeted Jack effusively and had us come in for tea. It was evident the two had known each other for some time. In the course of conversation, we learned that her husband was on a trip and would not be returning for a week or so. The small talk went on for about 15 minutes when Jack told her it was time for us to leave. I thanked the lady for her hospitality and started for the door. As I did so, I heard Jack tell her he would be back later to take her to dinner. I was sure he had more than dinner in mind—this guy was some operator.

We now headed for the Grand Hotel. On arrival, we walked into the lobby to see what was taking place. Three American nurses stood huddled in a small semi-circle looking very downcast. Jack breezed over, introduced himself, and asked what the nature of their problem might be. Seems they were on short leave and had been unable to secure a room at the hotel, as it was booked solid. They were agonizing over the fact that they would be forced to cut their leave short and return to base. Jack assured them he could help.

With this, he went up to the front desk, which was being run by an American sergeant. When he asked, he was told the one remaining open room was reserved for a lieutenant colonel so and so. Jack asked, "Did you say a lieutenant colonel?" When the sergeant answered in the affirmative, Jack told him that room would do fine and that he would take it. The sergeant was obviously in a quandary—"What the hell do I do now? I've got one room and it's reserved for a lieutenant colonel and here's this full bull demanding the room." Bowing to the immediacy of the problem, he finally slid the register over to Jack along with a key to the room. Signing the register with a flourish, he took the key and returned to the nurses.

"Ladies, your room, courtesy of Jack Carter." He told them he would stop by the next day and take the three of them to lunch.

Within 15 minutes we departed for the Bengal Air Depot, home for the ATSC. En route to the officers' quarters, we drove past a mile or so of airfield on which every type of airplane in the CBI inventory was parked while undergoing either maintenance or modification. It looked like Wright Field (later to become Wright Patterson Air Force Base). I had no previous knowledge as to the magnitude of this facility.

We turned into a drive leading to the officers' club, which looked for all the world like a stateside mansion. Off to the right on a beautifully manicured lawn was a second building, a stately two story structure. This was the officers' quarters. We checked in at the office and a houseboy led us to our rooms; Jack on the first floor and me on the second. Jack told me to meet him in the bar in about 15 minutes.

I was flabbergasted on seeing my quarters. I had a huge bedroom with a canopy-covered, four-poster, king sized bed, several chairs and a very expensive looking writing desk. The room was at least fourteen by sixteen feet in size and had a full-width balcony. My private bath had a Roman style sunken tub. Just a tiny bit fancier than the small, adobe room with bunk beds that I shared with three others in Yangkai. A man could become accustomed to these surroundings very easily.

Moments later, I walked across the beautiful lawn and entered the "O" club (officers' club). Hollywood couldn't have done a better job. Softly lighted and beautifully decorated, the club offered a delightful haven from the hot Indian sun. Jack had beaten me to the club. He was seated near the entrance and was being served a frosty drink by a very large Sikh in a snow-white uniform with red turban and matching red waist sash. I ordered a scotch and soda as I sank down in the very comfortable chair. The Sikh waiter trotted off to the huge mahogany bar as my eyes took in the rest of the club. Beyond where we were seated was the dining room with a teak wood floor inlaid in a herringbone fashion. The dining room was very large, capable of accommodating several hundred in a single seating. It was obviously used for dancing as well as dining, as I saw an orchestra section at the opposite end. Without question, the "O" club and quarters were carryovers from the glory days of the British Empire. "Real tough war these guys are fighting here," I thought.

I still couldn't believe all this was happening to me and said as much to Jack. "Must be great to be a full colonel," I said.

"Hells bells, Slim, you probably out rank me," he said with that now very familiar grin. "What is your permanent rank?"

"I'm a temporary first lieutenant and permanent second lieutenant in the reserve," I replied.

"Would you believe I am a permanent master sergeant?" he asked. "I have twenty years of active duty behind me and was serving as a demolition expert in North Africa when they gave me this assignment." He went on to tell me he had been given a brevet promotion to colonel to allow him to carry out his stay.

That famous grin flashed once more as he said, "I'm enjoying the hell out of this and am going to milk it for all it's worth. I know I'll be reverting to sergeant, perhaps as soon as I get back to Africa but if not then, certainly at the end of the war."

We spent the next half hour or so in small talk before saying our farewells and wishing each other well. For me, this had been one of the most interesting experiences of my life.

Later, as I sat alone drinking gin and tonic while eating a gourmet steak dinner, the permanent party officers began drifting into the dining room. A great many were accompanied by beautiful Anglo-Indian girls attired in full length evening gowns. A white tuxedo clad, swing orchestra was playing ala Glenn Miller for their dancing pleasure. As I had thought earlier, this was indeed a very grim war that these Air Corps ground-pounder types were fighting here in Bangalore. I didn't fully appreciate just how grim it was until later when I was in the John. There I heard two captains griping about the old man's latest orders. It seems the tyrant was going to put a crimp in their style by eliminating the "one officer per Jeep" policy long in existence and directing that from this day forth, two officers must now share a single Jeep.

On hearing their complaints I almost choked in disgust and muttered something like, "Poor little kids. That mean old colonel is taking your toys from you. How do you make out with your date when your buddy and his date are sitting on the back seat of your Jeep?"

I think the only thing that kept them from clobbering me on the spot was my A-2 flight jacket complete with the Flying Tiger and Eagle Squadron patches and the raunchy looking "100 mission" hat under my arm. They probably thought, "Just another one of those undisciplined, ill-mannered and sloppily-dressed thugs from China about whom 'Vinegar' Joe Stillwell is constantly chastising Chennault."

Following breakfast the next morning, I caught a flight to Karachi and then traveled the last five to ten miles to Malir, where I would spend several weeks sharing a small room with "Whispering Ray" Bohannon and W. O. Powell—my brief taste of how the other half lives put behind me for all time.

JUNGLE JIM

It was the spring of 1944. During one of several trips I was to make between India and China this year, I was forced to lay over in Chabua for about a week while waiting for weather and traffic to clear. As some might recall, one of the permanent party types at Chabua collected reptiles, which he housed in one of the bashas. At this particular time, his collection included one very large python, a dozen or more Russell Vipers and a beautiful King Cobra measuring ten to twelve feet in length. Rumor had it that the collector was, in civilian life, an assistant curator at a California zoo, who regularly shipped reptiles from India to the U.S. In any event, his collection was fascinating and I visited the basha several times to view his cold-blooded pets. One day, tiring of visiting the "Snake Pit," I walked to the nearby river with a first lieutenant infantry officer. He was armed with a carbine while my trusty Colt 45 (complete with ivory grips) was snug in my shoulder holster.

As we walked along the river bank, a stick measuring about 30 inches in length and about one inch in diameter floated past our position. At this point, my infantry companion whipped up his carbine and triggered off several shots at the stick. Although his rounds were very close, none hit the stick. At a point when the stick was about 50 feet downstream of our position, I said, "Watch this," pulling out my 45 as I spoke. Taking very deliberate aim, I fired once. The stick leaped into the air and fell in two pieces back into the river. I was stunned—it was a 1,000 to one shot—pure horse s...t luck. Recovering from my surprise quickly, I held the barrel close to my mouth and blew away the imaginary smoke. Mouth agape, my companion asked where I had learned to shoot like that. I very casually mentioned that all air corps types were trained in the "Billy the Kid" method of shooting and that I was indeed one of the poorer shots in the corps. His look was one of total awe.

During this same stay at Chabua, it was rumored that two other transients, tiring of the same movie every night, had walked to another base several miles distant where a different film was being shown. One was allegedly armed with an M-1 while the other supposedly carried a carbine. It was said that on their return to Chabua, they heard a noise on the opposite side of the row of bushes they were paralleling. When they stopped walking, the noise was not heard. After several such stops, one of the individuals was said to have leaned over the bush and shone his flashlight at the source. There, frozen by the light, was a huge Bengal tiger.

While he held his now badly shaking flashlight, the other took panic stricken aim with his M-1 and emptied it in the general direction of the huge burning eyes. The rumor had it that this was almost a record size kill and that, in all probability, this was the same tiger credited with having killed some twenty or more natives. True?—who knows? At any rate, it spiced up the conversation for the next several days.

Several years later, following my return to the states, I told these three totally unrelated tales to a favorite uncle—the snakes, the floating stick and, finally, the tiger. His retelling of the stories to his children and others who would listen was unbelievable. In a dead serious manner, he would tell of his nephew Jim walking through the jungle and encountering a huge king cobra which he dispatched with a single shot through the head.

On other occasions, it would be the story of nephew Jim encountering the largest Bengal tiger on record and killing the beast with a single well-placed shot in the eye. The truly amazing aspect is that these feats were supposedly accomplished when I was armed with nothing more than my trusty old 45.

To my cousins and other equally gullible listeners, I was Frank Buck, Sgt. York, Buffalo Bill and Wyatt Earp wrapped up in one mighty hunter. I am certain that my occasional wearing of the safari jacket, Karachi boots and pith helmet which I acquired during my stay in India did little to refute these outrageous tales.

ANN SHERIDAN'S
VISIT TO YANGKAI

During my stay in Yangkai, we were entertained by a number of Hollywood celebrities. Among these much appreciated performers were Ben Blue, Pat O'Brien, Keenan Wynn, Paulette Goddard and Jinx Falkenburg of modeling fame. I had been sent back to Malir Air Base on temporary duty during June of '44. It was in Chabua, on my return trip to Yangkai where I saw Paulette Goddard. She, too, was waiting for a hop across the Hump. I assumed that she visited Yangkai during her swing through China but that might not have been the case. In any event, the one who stands out in my mind almost 50 years later was Ann Sheridan—the former Texas school teacher turned sex symbol.

In anticipation of the "sweater girl's" visit, one of our more artistic squadron mates painted a beautiful picture of her on the side of one of our newer B-25s and dubbed the aircraft "The Sheridan Express." Never let it be said that the 22nd wasn't appreciative of the fairer sex.

By the time of her visit, I had become assistant transportation officer. The "old man" had been concerned about the idle time we fly boys enjoyed between missions. He dictated that we assume some sort of ground duty to carry out those days when we weren't flying. This would keep us out of mischief. Being a street-smart kid from Detroit, this cagey bombardier/navigator immediately volunteered to become assistant transportation officer. My mother hasn't raised any idiots—this move gave me access to wheels.

On the day of the Sheridan visit, I was sitting alone in the motor pool, having given the go-ahead to the on-duty drivers to make a bee line for the theater and the good seats. The phone

323

rang—It was the base C.O. He was a small, wizened-up lieutenant colonel—a World War I retread.

The good colonel directed that I send a staff car to his quarters to pick him up and deliver him to the flight line, where he would greet Miss Sheridan. After she christened the Sheridan Express, we would drive the party back to his quarters where they would freshen up and have a drink before heading out to the theater. I informed the colonel that my drivers were all presently at the theater. Somewhat testily he asked, "You drive, don't you lieutenant?—I will expect you in five minutes." Within five minutes I was behind the wheel of a command car (over-sized Jeep with a canvas top).

I stood rather quietly in the background as the colonel fawned all over Annie. The party then climbed into my command car. The colonel, Miss Sheridan and a starlet I have long since forgotten, occupied the rear seat. I was joined in the front by Major Melvin Douglas, who was then a special services officer. We made the scheduled stop at the colonel's quarters where I was told to remain at the car until their return.

It was obvious that Miss Sheridan was very testy and out-of-sorts—The food?—The grueling schedule?—Lousy beds?—Who knows why. In any event, she was less than awe-inspiring on that

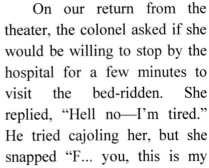

particular day.

On our return from the theater, the colonel asked if she would be willing to stop by the hospital for a few minutes to visit the bed-ridden. She replied, "Hell no—I'm tired." He tried cajoling her, but she snapped "F... you, this is my trip and I just want to get the hell out of here as fast as possible." Whenever the colonel, now rather timidly, asked another question, he was greeted with yet another string of four letter words. Douglas turned to me and observed, "Salty, ain't she?"

It had been raining for several days. As we traversed the road which led from the base down the mountain to the landing strip below, the car slid on the mud. I braked and we came to a stop with the right front wheel about six inches from the unguarded edge.

From this vantage point in the right front seat, Douglas peered almost straight down for about 100 feet. Turning to me with a grin he said, "You believe in cutting it pretty close, don't you lieutenant?" A few more inches and I might have terminated two of Hollywood's reigning super stars.

I was happy when that day came to an end.

A WINNER WITH
CANADIAN CLUB

It seems the squadron had, somehow or other, come into possession of a very limited supply of Canadian Club. As I recall, there were five bottles in all. How does one distribute five bottles of booze to an entire squadron? How about a lottery where the names of all are placed in a hat and then five are drawn as winners? It seemed like a great idea, so the drawing was held. Yours truly was off on a mission when the names were placed in the hat (or whatever), shaken about a bit and five were withdrawn. Bob Burnham was one of the lucky five, as was Jim White. (Someone must have been honest as hell—how would I have known whether or not my name had been drawn?)

In any event, on my return from the mission, I was given a bottle of Canadian Club. Not being a drinker at the time, I decided to share the bottle with some of the others in the immediate vicinity. In rather short order, the last drop of CC was drained from the bottle. Now what? Someone suggested we visit Bob Burnham. If you recall, Canadian Club is bottled in a dark brown bottle—if you fill an empty with water, Voila! it looks like a full bottle of CC. The plot was hatched. I knew that Bob, like me, was not much of a drinker, meaning he would not be greatly harmed by our nefarious scheme.

Four or five of us headed for Bob's room. He was not in sight, but his CC was. I quickly swapped my bottle of water for his booze. We walked outside his room and ran into Bob as he was returning from the head.

I told Bob that I was about to share my CC with some of the others and suggested he do the same with his. He very readily agreed to do so. He went into his room and returned with the bottle. I suggested he take the first drink from his bottle or risk not having any at all, with this thirsty group of pirates standing about just waiting to pounce on the jug. He questioned why the seal was broken on the bottle, but was assured that was purely accidental and would have no effect on the liquor.

He tipped it back and took a slug. Putting the bottle down, with a quizzical look, he said, "Gosh, that was pretty weak." For those of you who might not fully recall, Bob was a slim, blond, naive kid from Utah, with a look of perpetual wonderment on his face. I suggested he take another drink, which he did with the same results—"Gosh, I really think someone has been fooling around with my whiskey." I told him that was an unspeakable crime, and the miscreant should probably be hung from the nearest tree. He nodded in agreement.

I then broke the seal on his bottle and said, "Here, you take the first drink from mine." I then suggested he have a second drink. After one circuit amongst the guys standing around, Bob's bottle was also emptied as quickly as had been mine.

Bob was effusive in thanking me—"Gee, Jim, you are one great guy." I never did have the heart to tell him of my duplicity.

Carl A. Gibson
IT PAYS TO FASTEN
YOUR SEAT BELT

Here is a story about the monsoons while flying out of Chakulia, India, in '43. We were to bomb near Mandalay, the Japanese division headquarters in Burma. It was one of the worst storms we had flown formation through. I had a hard time as a wingman keeping my eyes on the lead ship. Even though we were flying as close as was safe, the heavy rains would blur out the lead ship so that some ships separated out only to rejoin again in a clear rendezvous later on. One ship flown by Victor "Smitty" Smith did just that, only to end up in a thunderhead, as told by Frank "Mac" Majesky, the copilot.

According to his story, they must have ended up in an inverted spin because of the violence inside the cockpit. His head was being battered against the window casing but he had his seat belt on, which saved him. He was trying to get his chute buckled on, which some of us didn't do until we thought it was necessary. But Smitty, the pilot, wasn't buckled up and Mac watched him fly out the top hatch without his chute.

Mac claims he had fastened one leg strap and the violence was so bad he unfastened the seat belt so he could jump before the plane hit the jungle of the Chin Hills. The next thing he knew was that he was floating down with one leg connected to the

Editor's note: Carl Gibson was a member of the 491st Bomb Squadron, the 22nd's sister squadron, located at the same base as the 22nd, and flew the same type of airplane on many of the same missions as the 22nd.

chute, upside down. As he was trying to reach up for the straps to prevent falling out of the chute, he noticed the twin rudder tail assembly was floating down over him in falling-leaf fashion. He envisioned the next pass would probably get him or the parachute, but it slid off to the side and he landed high in the trees. He remembers that the growth in the trees was so thick that he literally had to crawl down the tree and through the limbs to get to the underbrush. Then he wondered how he could get through the brush, until he lucked out (so he thought) to find an opening big enough for him to crouch and crawl through, but he happened upon a big animal foot print in a muddy spot on the trail. He reasoned that could only be a tiger track, so he climbed back up the tree where he landed.

After a while he heard noises of men coming through with machetes, cutting a path through the jungle. Finally, he could see them through the dense brush from his perch up in the tree. Then he had his next worry. The men looked like they had Japanese soldiers' uniforms. But after a closer examination he saw they were mix-matched uniforms unlike what spit-and-polish soldiers would wear. He thought  these must be Chin Hills people who we believed hated the Japanese. We had heard stories how, in the past, Japanese pirates

would raid the Chin villages for their beautiful women and bring them back to Japan. So Mac believed these were Chin people looking for the downed plane and crew. These Chins had acquired their Japanese duds somehow and were using them for dress in these far out villages.

Well, Mac was in luck. They retrieved him from the tree and jungle and brought him to the chieftain in a settlement nearby. In the jungle, the natives had heard that a good bounty would be paid for the return of downed service men found after falling from the sky. So Mac was to receive a welcome he never expected. The chief set him on his throne and had all the young maidens bringing him fruit and vegetables, which they set at his feet. Mac just accepted them and waved each maiden away as they deposited their wares at his feet. Afterwards, when the last maiden had passed, the chief became irate. Mac didn't understand the language or the customs and was beside himself until one of the British interpreters showed up to inform Mac that he had refused all the chief's wives that were being offered. This was a big insult in that culture.

At the 491st squadron base we got the word that Majesky was safe and that I was to fly to Chittagong to pick him up. It was hard to get him into the B-25 to fly him back to Chakulia. But after three months he was back to flying missions again, with wild stories to tell.

He became a close friend of mine, as had been his pilot Smitty at the time. We went through transition flight training in the B-25 at Columbia Air Base, South Carolina, in '42 and '43.

Editor: This mission was described from the official records by McKay Nelson of the 491st Bomb Squadron as follows:

"One aircraft and crew was missing from the mission of October 30th (1943) when nine B-25s successfully attacked the barracks at Meiktila. Buildings were hit and fires started, but complete observation of results was impossible due to dirt and debris covering the area where the bomb hits were scored. Aircraft No. 66 disappeared shortly after leaving the scene of the attack. The weather was extremely bad. The aircraft was piloted by Lt. Victor Smith. Others in the crew were Lt. Frank Majesky, Daniel O'Connor, S/Sgts. Joe Ayoub, Stanley Penkul and Donald Muntzinger.

"On November 6, 1943," McKay Nelson continued, "Lt. Frank Majesky, who had been reported missing in action following a squadron mission in Burma in late October, returned to the squadron. Majesky was the only one of the missing crew able to bail out. The others are believed to have been killed when the aircraft crashed."

UPSTAGING THE
FIGHTER SQUADRON

Even though we were over there helping the Chinese people fight the Japanese, we were constantly harassed by the Chinese guerrillas. I remember one night being awakened by guerrillas raiding our radio station in Yangkai. When we sent a truck to Kunming, somebody had to ride shotgun because of the attacks along the road back. It was said the bandits would put a blockage on the road to make the truck stop. Then the bandits would attack.

I remember one time when I was ferrying a couple of GI's to Kunming to catch a flight home to the USA, which turned out to be comical. After I dropped off the deportees at Kunming, I ran into a crew which was to truck our supplies back to Yangkai and they asked me if I would fly cover for them at the mountain pass where these raids generally occurred. I asked them what time they would be reaching that troublesome pass. They told me and I said I would delay my flight long enough so I would meet them at the appointed time.

Then, in the meantime a flight surgeon, a major, approached me for a ride to Yangkai so that he could get in on the table stakes card game that went on every pay day.

I told him I had to wait a couple of hours to check on my truck obligation. We waited over a couple of drinks and lots of conversation and he remarked that he was with a fighter squadron and that those pilots were really hot pilots. So to make a long story short, I loaded him on the B-25H I was flying and set him in the copilot's seat with no controls where he could get a first-hand and close-up view of the ride he was going to have. I then told him we were going to meet the truck at the narrow pass where the bandits would be waiting.

When we got there I wanted to get a real close view of the situation to see if any bandits were lurking in the shadows ahead of the truck. This required some treetop-level flying with the mountains shooting up on both sides.

We couldn't see anything but trees, and we were close enough to count the leaves on the trees and the rough end of the gravel road. After buzzing low, then climbing up around the mountain a few times before the truck arrived, we then waved them on with the "all clear" sign.

I didn't think any more of it until we arrived at Yangkai, when we were met by some of the high rollers at the airstrip. This major said to them, "I'll never brag about my hot pilots to a Mitchell bomber pilot again. I'm glad to get my feet on solid ground again."

I have a snapshot of the two men I took to Kunming but I don't remember their names and I don't know how the major made out in the card game, for I never saw him again. It turned out to be an uneventful trip, as there were no raids by bandits for excitement. It does point out, however, the harassment those bandits caused us, along with low rations and the shortage of gas in fighting the Japanese.

Felix M. "Phil" Speciale
MISSING IN ACTION
AT HAINAN ISLAND

On April 15, 1944, orders came to headquarters that a large fleet of Japanese troop ships and destroyers were in Suma Bay, Hainan Island. Due to thick fog, our crew delayed takeoff until around midnight, with Lt. Jerry Miller at the controls.

We hugged the beach about 100 feet above ground and received heavy ack-ack fire. Once we crossed the island, we found all the troopships and destroyers sitting there like ducks.

Lt. Miller chose to drop our 500 pound bombs one at a time. During our runs, our plane was hit several times. At that time we noticed other planes that joined us in our bombing runs.

Heading home towards Tangse we were freezing when Lt. Miller called out to check the bomb bay, as the plane felt like it was dragging. Looking down into the bomb bay I found a 500 pound bomb with only half of a shackle engaged.

Without thinking, I placed the bomb bay cable around me and took out the steel axe, with the flight engineer and radioman holding onto the cable. I was lowered into the bomb bay. In turn, with the steel axe, I cut loose the 500 pound bomb at approximately 500 feet above the bay. When it hit, it exploded and I thought I was going to be a drowned rat.

335

On the way back to our base, the overcast was severe and the damaged plane left little decision room for Lt. Miller. However, there was a small hole in the cloud-covered sky. Lt. Miller gave us a choice. Either bail out or we would dip our wing into the center of the hole and dive down, which we did. We broke out into a valley and "Yea! Rice paddies."

Lt. Miller, without wheels, dropped his tail and came to a sliding halt within a two-foot wall of a rice paddy. All got out safely and we walked in by April 25, 1944.

Our crew was Lt. Jerry Miller, pilot; Lt. William Bartholic, navigator-bombardier; Sgt. William Keegin, flight engineer, Sgt. Melvin Braemer, radio operator; and myself, Sgt. Felix "Phil" Speciale, gunner.

Chapman M. Hale, Jr.

AN UNUSUAL TRIP
WITH MAJOR ARTHER

I remember Major Arther, intelligence officer for the 341st Bomb Group. This is not a "blood and guts" episode—just an acknowledgement of a very fine man.

A couple of us, including Lee Roy Horton, visited Major Arther at the 341st HQ for a long forgotten reason. He, being a fine fellow, invited us to visit the "Temple of 1000 Gods," or something to that effect.

He had a Jeep and gasoline so we departed for the distant mountains. After a few miles he announced that he was hungry and we should get something to eat—with us being out in the "boondocks."

He found a Chinese hut—a hovel— and proceeded to talk the lady of the house into serving us for some price. Of course the hovel was unbelievably primitive, filthy and smelly. She served each of us a bowl of some kind of noodles, which of course we greenhorns were totally unable to eat. Major Arther ate his portion with gusto and had a good laugh at our lack of appetite and discomfort.

Following the "gourmet" meal, we continued far into the mountains. At our destination, the city of Kunming and the lake were far below our feet. There were enormous caves where the Chinese has stashed away their treasures—hopefully hiding them from the expected Japanese occupation of the city.

Some caves were filled with thousands of books from libraries. The other caves, which were of the most interest, were huge and filled with figurines and idols representing their religion and a lot of other things, I suppose. There were hundreds upon hundreds of these idols of every imaginable configuration, size and color.

I particularly remember some Buddhas that were enormous, probably twelve to fifteen feet high and four to six feet wide, and

of course in gold. This was quite an experience, as I had never heard of that place before or since, as I had a sheltered life.

This was an unusual and enjoyable experience. I appreciated the effort of that genial gentleman Major Arther to give us such an unusual trip.

EPILOGUE

Forty-two years after the end of World War II, in 1987, a group of veterans of the 22nd Bomb Squadron met in St. Louis, MO, and held a reunion. Arrangements were made by John W. Boyd, a radio operator-gunner with the 22nd, whose B-25 had been shot down on a mission to Meiktila, Burma, in 1943, and who had spent the rest of the war in a Japanese prisoner of war camp. John is known as the "father" of the 22nd Bomb Squadron Association. He had a successful career in the real estate business in Mayfield, Kentucky, where he and his wife Ruby lived. He served on the city council and was mayor of Mayfield. John passed away in 2007.

At the 1987 reunion, the 22nd Bomb Squadron Association was founded and Wilmer E. McDowell was elected its first president. He continued to serve the association as its membership chairman until his death in the year 2001. "Wil" was pilot of one of twenty-six B-25s that flew first from Florida to India in 1942. Annual reunions have been held since 1989.

One of the functions of the 22nd Bomb Squadron Association has been to publish a quarterly newsletter. Steve Stankiewicz began contributing stories in 1993; his first was "Nepalese Vacation, Shangri La?" In 1997, his stories appeared in the squadron history book *Eagles, Bulldogs & Tigers.* After the war, Steve married "his girl" Frankie. He remained in the air force, following which he served with the U. S. Postal Service until his retirement in New Jersey. Steve passed away in 1999, but his stockpile of stories remains for the public to enjoy.

Also in 1993, Jim White began submitting his stories to the 22nd Bomb Squadron newsletter. His first was "Ann Sheridan's Visit to Yangkai." His stories, too, have continued through the years, appearing in the newsletter and in the squadron's history, *Eagles, Bulldogs & Tigers*. Jim, too, married his childhood sweetheart, Evelyn, and then was called back into the service during the Korean War, remaining with the air force until retirement as a lieutenant colonel. Jim passed away at his home in Annandale, Virginia, in the year 2001.

The story "Ann Sheridan's Visit to Yangkai" was illustrated with caricatures drawn by John A. Johns, who had been a pilot with the 22nd Bomb Squadron. He then became a regular illustrator of the stories of Stankiewicz, White and others. John made a career out of his art work. After the war, he joined the art staff of the Pittsburgh Press, then took on the job of president of the Art Institute of Pittsburgh, and retired as president emeritus of that institute. John passed away in 2005, but his brilliant art work will live on.

Wendell Hanson served as president of the 22nd Bomb Squadron Association in 1993. In his memoir entitled *The Brotherhood of World War II*, he wrote, "This essay is written to that great, great-grandchild who may have the desire in the year 2101 to look back at a time in history when the world was on the brink of disaster. Millions and more millions of the earth's people were killed and I was one of the survivors." Ten stories from Wendell's memoirs appear in this book. He has had a distinguished life, first in the military after the war, then in real estate and as a state senator in South Dakota. He and his wife, Helen, live in a suburb of Sioux Falls, SD.

David Hayward, the editor of this book, has been Secretary-Treasurer of the 22nd Bomb Squadron Association since 1989. In that role, he has accumulated many stories and materials that were contributed by members of the squadron. Recognizing that these materials are just too good to be lost, he has combined them into three collections in addition to this book: the quarterly newsletters, the squadron's history entitled *Eagles, Bulldogs & Tigers*, and the videotape *Eagles, Bulldogs & Tigers in Action*. Dave Hayward is a retired petroleum engineer, living with his wife Jeanne in Huntington Beach, California.

Jay Percival lived in Lompoc, CA, "Tommy" Thompson in Burlington, NC, Carl Gibson also in Burlington, NC, Phil Speciale in Henderson, NV, and Bill Van Vleck in Clearwater, FL. Chapman Hale currently lives in Kingsport, TN.

One of the works of art that John A. Johns contributed to the 22nd Bomb Squadron Association is this drawing:

Its title is from the song, "You are the Wind Beneath my Wings." John gives credit to Michelangelo, as this work was inspired by the painting of God on the ceiling of the Sistine Chapel in Rome.

Those men who proudly flew in the B-25s and those who provided the essential ground support, who were fortunate to have survived the constant dangers of World War II in the China-Burma-India Theater, were indeed grateful for the wind beneath their wings and Almighty God who made possible their survival.

Lightning Source UK Ltd.
Milton Keynes UK
UKOW02f0855080716

277903UK00002B/308/P